VOLCKER

PORTRAIT OF
THE MONEY MAN

VOLCKER

PORTRAIT OF
THE MONEY MAN

WILLIAM R. NEIKIRK

CONGDON & WEED, INC.
New York • Chicago

Library of Congress Cataloging-in-Publication Data

Neikirk, William.
  Volcker, portrait of the money man.

    1. Volcker, Paul A.   2. Economists—United States—
Biography.   3. Board of Governors of the Federal
Reserve System (U.S.)—Officials and employees—
Biography.   4. United States—Economic policy—1971–1981.
5. United States—Economic policy—1981-   .   I. Title.
HB119.V6N45   1987   332.1'1'0924 [B]   87-19953
ISBN 0-86553-178-1
ISBN 0-8092-0178-1 (Contemporary Books)

Published by Congdon & Weed, Inc.
A subsidiary of Contemporary Books, Inc.
298 Fifth Avenue, New York, New York 10001
Distributed by Contemporary Books, Inc.
180 North Michigan Avenue, Chicago, Illinois 60601

Published simultaneously in Canada by Beaverbooks, Ltd.
195 Allstate Parkway, Valleywood Business Park
Markham, Ontario L3R 4T8 Canada

To Ruth Ann
For Ruth Snapp Clary
Money isn't everything.

CONTENTS

PREFACE

The first time I met Paul A. Volcker, he was undersecretary of the Treasury for monetary affairs, and I was a young Associated Press correspondent assigned to the Treasury. It was 1970, and I had just unsuccessfully resisted being sent to the Treasury to cover economics for the AP. I viewed it as only a temporary assignment, a stepping-stone to cover politics, the White House, Congress, or some other beat I fancied as more glamorous.

I remember struggling with both the jargon and the substance of this new beat, especially when I went to my first Volcker briefing. It was a quarterly "refunding" of Treasury debt, and Volcker presided over it with a confidence that I thought bordered on arrogance. I recall how he was telling us of his aim to lengthen the maturities of Treasury debt and put it on a sounder footing. This was a year in which the deficit was to reach $23 billion, about 10 percent of what it is today, yet debt worried Volcker even then. I left this press conference with two impressions: this was going to be a hard beat, and Volcker was very, very good.

Volcker had not honed his communications skills in those days and did not care much if reporters failed to understand him the first time around. He was not especially keen on helping us do our jobs, preferring to work quietly behind the scenes to do his.

My UPI colleague, Norman Kempster, now with the *Los Angeles Times*, had a nice little phrase with a double meaning about his tall frame: Paul Volcker, he said, was the only man who could talk down to you and over your head at the same time.

Volcker was so good at his job that he was, in essence, running the Treasury Department in those days. The Treasury secretary was David M. Kennedy, a soft-spoken Chicago banker who was inexperienced in international economics and politics, and Volcker helped fill that void to a large extent, except for maybe the political side of the equation.

The political void was filled early in 1971 when President Nixon named John B. Connally, the swashbuckling Texan, as secretary of the Treasury. Connally was a man of action and quickly moved the administration to accept wage-price controls. With Volcker as his idea man, he also persuaded Nixon to close the gold window and no longer let foreign governments exchange their dollars for gold. The latter move launched Volcker's high-profile career in international economics.

I was intrigued by him then. He would clumsily stroll out of some big international meeting, his head towering above all the rest. He was easy to spot but difficult to question, avoiding eye contact as well as he could and trying to brush us off with a flip remark. Most of the time, this tactic worked. Volcker never gave us much news in these public confrontations. Privately, he was a good briefer, although some of my colleagues found him a bit intimidating.

Those were exciting times to be an economics reporter in Washington because the whole international monetary system was in turmoil and, we thought at the time, in the process of being reformed. Volcker, we all knew, was the brains behind this reformation, but he kept his distance from the press in those days, except when he thought an anonymous leak or tip would serve his purpose. Largely because economics became one of the big, lasting stories of the 1970s, the number of economics reporters in Washington increased dramatically.

When I decided to tackle the job of writing a book on Volcker, the first thing that crossed my mind was how his presence, and the role he played in the early 1970s, influenced my decision to remain in the field of economics writing. The second thing was how he had been such a pivotal figure in the lives of ordinary Americans for so long. The end of the Bretton Woods monetary system in the early 1970s still influences the international monetary system and the value of the dollar in ways that most Americans only dimly perceive.

What Volcker is most known for, however, is his tough action in controlling inflation from 1979 to 1982. I decided that any book on him should really focus on these years, since his work during that period was his main contribution to the economic life of this country.

These were terrible years for the American economy, a time of painful transition from high to low inflation. In this regard, Volcker liked to think of himself as a surgeon, but he developed critics on the left and on the right who thought of him as a hapless butcher in the way he used monetary policy. During this critical period, there were many calls from Congress and the White House for him to ease up. As people suffered from high interest rates caused by Fed policies, Volcker became a target for the public policymakers in Congress and the White House. He was criticized at one time or another for poor judgment, stubbornness, and a lack of compassion. Some found him highly manipulative and disingenuous in the way he tried to divert criticism from the Federal Reserve and his policies. Some didn't like the way he threw his weight around in Washington, all the while hiding in a shroud of secrecy. To some, he could be cold and intimidating.

One would have thought that someone who had tackled such a big job in conflict with the agendas of so many powerful people would have aroused strong emotional reaction and doubt about his integrity. Yet, in my interviews with Volcker's friends and associates, as well as his critics, I found only a handful who felt a personal animosity against him or did not think that he had high integrity.

I'll admit to liking Volcker. He is probably the most secretive man I've ever met and certainly one of the most difficult to get to know. But I found in my talks with him that he is not vindictive and, in fact, frequently invites his critics in for conversation, unless they are uncivil (as some of them are). Like most complex human beings, he can be gruff, and he can be warm. I found his use of the language precise and his interpretation of the economic events of the times vivid and on the mark.

Some of his critics, like monetarist economist Milton Friedman, try to deemphasize his significance by calling him a bureaucrat and civil servant. This attitude is based on the notion that Fed chairmen pretty much do the bidding of the president in power. I think this interpretation understates and even demeans Volcker's importance in conquering inflation and his role in the international monetary turmoil of the 1970s. He was far more than a bureaucrat or civil servant; he was calling the shots to a large extent.

Most people do not find Volcker funny. Over the years, I often agreed, but he does have a quick, pungent wit and a way of pulling your leg. I liked the story that Robert Solomon of the Brookings Institution told about him. They were at a big international meeting on the dollar crisis in 1970 when the representative from the Netherlands made a proposal to help solve the trouble. "And how many divisions do the Dutch have?" Volcker responded.

Self-confidence is an essential quality for a central banker. The markets can sense wimpish behavior and rhetoric. Volcker can be accused of many things, but rarely of being soft. This need often brought out some unattractive personality traits. He doesn't suffer fools gladly, and he doesn't feel the constant need to explain himself. He became a master of obfuscation when testifying on Capitol Hill, preferring generalities over specifics. He was one of the best turf battlers in Washington, which boasts some pretty good ones; he fought to preserve the Fed's power in regulating banks when the Reagan administration sought to eliminate overlapping and confusing authority and consolidate it into one super-regulator.

Sometimes he infuriated staff members by refusing to communicate on the one hand or driving them too hard on the other. But they appreciated his contribution, by and large. As one told me, "Thank God he's been around for the last eight years. I'd hate to think what the economy would be like without him."

Volcker isn't perfect and wasn't the only person who could have run the Fed skillfully in those critical eight years of the American economy. But the important thing is that we could have done much worse.

Economist Alan Greenspan recommended to President Reagan in 1983 that Volcker be reappointed to a second term. As Greenspan explained his recommendation, "While there may have been a lot of people who had the capability of doing as well as Paul, he had all the connections, knew all the people, and had all the relationships internationally. That's an invaluable resource which you just don't throw away." Greenspan made these remarks before he knew that he would, in 1987, be chosen as Volcker's successor.

The Volcker era may have come to an end in U.S. economic history, but not the impact of his policies and his personality. Greenspan knows that Volcker gained credibility the hard way and, before his term is over, that he may have to do the same.

—William Neikirk
June 1987

ACKNOWLEDGMENTS

My thanks go to Paul Volcker's family for generously giving me time and background on his life. In this regard, I am especially grateful to Barbara Volcker and James (Jimmy) Volcker for their insights and good humor. I am also grateful to Ruth Volcker and Virginia Volcker Streitfield, Paul's sisters, for filling in important gaps and trying to paint a picture of his life in Teaneck, New Jersey, and to his daughter, Janice, for her frank assessments of her father.

Volcker's friends also were extremely helpful. This list includes Robert Kavesh, Edward Yeo, and Gerald Corrigan, the last two being close fishing partners of the chairman. Robert Roosa took time from his busy schedule as well to provide details on Paul Volcker's career.

Peter Bakstansky, Corrigan's aide at the Federal Reserve Bank of New York, provided assistance, as did former New York Fed president Anthony Solomon.

Joseph R. Coyne, Volcker's assistant and one of the best economic reporters the Associated Press ever produced, was invaluable to me. Also helpful were former Fed governors Lyle Gramley and Nancy Teeters.

My thanks go out to my bosses, especially my managing editor, F. Richard Ciccone, for being so understanding during this project. My bureau chief, Nicholas Horrock, and my news editor, Randolph Murray, provided both encouragement and understanding.

I also am grateful to such friends as Art Pine of the *Wall Street Journal*, Peter Torday of Reuters, and Hobart Rowen of the *Washington Post* for encouragement, along with Michael Kilian in my own newspaper office at the *Chicago Tribune* Washington Bureau.

A special note of gratitude goes to my wife, Ruth, for putting up with the clutter around my Osborne computer and for my odd working hours. To my children, Christa, Greg, and John, I can only say thanks for the support.

Editor Clay Smudsky of Contemporary Books was constantly on the telephone with ideas and suggestions. He spurred me ahead.

Finally, to Paul Volcker himself, a special note of thanks. May you be rich one day.

VOLCKER
PORTRAIT OF
THE MONEY MAN

1
IN VOLCKER WE TRUST

     Anthony (Tony) Solomon was taking a relaxing swim in his pool on a steamy Saturday morning in the suburbs of Washington, DC, a therapy he perhaps needed in the wake of recent events. As undersecretary of the Treasury for monetary affairs, he had seen his government and his president, Jimmy Carter, desperately trying to come to grips with an economic and political crisis that threatened the administration's very existence.

     OPEC (Organization of Petroleum Exporting Countries) had once again raised oil prices, a move that would ignite inflationary growth, cripple world financial markets, and exacerbate the instability of the dollar. In his high-level Treasury post, the dollar was Solomon's chief concern and responsibility. Most of all, in July 1979, he wanted to avoid a collapse in the nation's currency, which was all too close to becoming reality.

     As part of his effort to regain the public's confidence, Carter, a day earlier, had told Treasury Secretary W. Michael Blumenthal that his services would no longer be

1

needed and turned to Federal Reserve Board Chairman G. William Miller to replace him. The markets had demonstrated absolutely no confidence in Miller's performance at the Fed, while Miller himself wasn't comfortable in the post and harbored political ambitions, hoping to be named as a vice presidential candidate on a Democratic ticket.

Carter's cabinet-shuffling was an effort to extricate himself from the deepest political crisis of his presidency, a crisis he tried to shake off with his ill-fated "malaise" speech. In that address, Carter explained that Americans suffered from a crisis of confidence. The speech was not well received by the public because it seemed that Carter was trying to pass off the blame to the people rather than where it belonged, on his administration.

As Solomon sought a respite from these swirling events, the poolside telephone rang. It was the president.

"He said he hoped that I would stay in my position at the Treasury, and, since Miller was going to be coming to the Treasury, he wanted me to recommend to him who should be the new chairman of the Fed," Solomon recalled.

"So I said to him, 'Paul Volcker.' And he said to me, 'Who's Paul Volcker?' "

After Solomon explained that Volcker was president of the Federal Reserve Bank of New York, Carter brought up another candidate he had in mind for Fed chairman. "Why not David Rockefeller?" he said, referring to the chairman of Chase Manhattan Bank and, ironically, one of Volcker's earlier mentors in the banking field.

"Because," Solomon told the president, "David doesn't have the technical understanding to conduct monetary policy and would, in my opinion, be murdered on the Hill [Congress] when he appeared to testify before .committees."

Carter replied that he didn't understand Solomon's comment about the required technical ability to run the

Fed: "Doesn't the Fed have a staff of technicians? Why does the chairman of the Fed have to have technical ability?"

"Unlike some other policy-making jobs," Solomon told Carter, "the chairman of the Federal Reserve must have the understanding of how the economy works and how monetary policy impacts on the economy. He must be able to preside over a very difficult decision-making process, and he must be able to articulate it very carefully because, more than any other single person, the markets are impacted by what he says."

Solomon's recommendation made a distinct impression on the embattled president, who promised Solomon he would interview Volcker. Although Carter didn't know of Volcker when he spoke to Solomon, he was to hear his name frequently in succeeding days as one influential financier after another told the president that Volcker was the best person to head up the central bank.

According to one official involved in the search committee for a new Fed chairman, Volcker got the best all-around marks from a wide variety of economists and financial and business leaders interviewed. In addition, his intellect and strong convictions appealed to Carter, who valued competence and technical expertise. "Carter felt compatible with him," said the official. "In terms of pure merit and substance, he stood above the crowd. He was highly regarded abroad, and he had experience at the New York Fed. With the kind of turmoil we had in the markets, you could argue that he would hit the ground running."

Still, Carter hesitated in selecting Volcker. Despite Solomon's flag of caution to Carter, David Rockefeller told biographer John D. Wilson that the president offered the job to him, an impression shared by many Carter aides. But Rockefeller turned it down, prompting Carter to question whether the great reputation of the Rockefeller family for public service was all it was cracked up to be.

In addition, administration officials at the time said that the president also dangled the Fed job before A. W. Clausen, president of the Bank of America.

What was being held against Volcker was both his well-known independent streak and his feeling that tight money was needed. Miller, who opposed the Volcker appointment internally, was worried about a recession. "There was a lot of tension internally about Volcker's views," the Carter official went on. "The president was inclined to go with Volcker, but several of us went in to see him and told him that it might not be the right thing. He may have better marks than the others, but that may be outweighed by the fact that he may not be a team player. At that point, Bill Miller was called in. The two of them [Carter and Miller] called Clausen. He was in California, having breakfast with his wife. They put the question to him: Would you be interested in the Fed? Clausen cupped his hand over the phone and said something like 'Hey, honey, do you want to go to Washington?' And she said, no, she didn't want to leave California."

Vice President Walter Mondale, who was in charge of the search for a new Fed chairman, said that while the president may have done some recruiting of his own, he was under the impression that the only real firm offer went to Volcker.

Rockefeller and Clausen were sounded out on the Treasury job as well and also declined that post, making Miller a third choice. Clausen did, however, come to Washington later to become president of the World Bank (a job, ironically, that Volcker turned down in 1986 when the Reagan administration offered it to him in an effort to oust him gently). Although Clausen, too, was well known internationally in 1979, he had none of the mystique and respect that appeared to surround Volcker. Volcker's reputation approached cult-like proportions, and it was to grow.

A COMPELLING PRAGMATISM

By 1979, Paul Adolph Volcker, Jr., had already established his reputation in international financial circles. In both height and demeanor, he commanded the respect of a de Gaulle. His six-foot seven-inch stature and towering intellect made him an imposing figure in public, intimidating politician and financier alike. The financial world remembered him as the chief architect of President Nixon's 1971 plan to end the system of fixed exchange rates for currencies that had existed since World War II. Even though he was not the top official in the Treasury Department during the Nixon years, the rest of the world treated him as if he were. He had helped manage the world economy through some difficult times, rubbing shoulders with the future presidents of West Germany (Helmut Schmidt) and France (Valery Giscard d'Estaing) in the process. Now he was being summoned again, this time to fight a raging inflation that threatened the very lifeblood of capitalism.

What was there about this man that was so compelling to the political and financial leaders of the world? It was not just his superb tactical handling of the 1971–73 dismantling of the world monetary system in favor of a new regime of floating exchange rates. Nor was it merely his reputation as a "hard-money man" who stressed the control of inflation and the credibility of one's national currency. It wasn't even his keen understanding of international economics. It was his undaunting pragmatic nature.

They loved his pragmatism, just as they loved his unpretentiousness. They were enamored of his ability to speak in profound generalities without revealing details, which meant to them that he possessed that bankerlike quality of being discreet. They loved his ability to diagnose trouble in the monetary system before others and to step in and manage a financial crisis almost better than anyone. They loved him because he talked their own language about the integrity of money and the dangers of debt. They loved the way he carried himself, high above the heads of others, puffing a cigar and moving straight ahead without meeting the eyes of lesser lights. They loved him because of an indefinable quality that exuded confidence and trustworthiness, the same principles that stand behind a country's money.

To them, Volcker seemed the closest thing to money itself, a money man who had very little of it. It is no wonder that journals of the day occasionally printed cartoons featuring a dollar with Volcker's picture in the center, with the caption "In Volcker we trust."

Volcker agonized over whether to take the Fed chair. His son, Jimmy, had cerebral palsy that affected his ability to walk. As a youngster, he had had a number of operations. He said that as a young man, there were many times in which he felt self-pity and lacked self-confidence. Volcker's wife, Barbara, suffered from diabetes and arthritis and did not want to return to Washington. She loved New York, calling it "the only place where I don't have an accent." It was not without pain that they reached an accord. He would take the job and commute to New York on weekends to see them. Barbara did not stand in Paul's way. It was, she said, the culmination of a long career in international economics.

There seemed little doubt that he would take the job, but Volcker sought the reaction of a few friends, including his former press aide at the Treasury, William R. Weber, now a Washington attorney. "When he left the Treasury, I remember asking him what his biggest disappointment was in those years, and he said, 'Not doing better on inflation.' When he called me before taking this job, I recalled what he had told me back then and told him, 'No position anywhere gives a greater chance of dealing with inflation than the Federal Reserve Board.' "

A less assured man might shrink from the task of solving, or even ameliorating, one of modern society's most intractable problems, a task that was bound to bring him into conflict with the political leaders of the time. Although Volcker is, to a great extent, a shy man in his personal relationships, he is not shy when it comes to belief in his own ability to accomplish tasks. "He is the most self-confident man I've ever met," said his wife. This quality others see as conceit, even arrogance.

The job he was about to take on was, as Solomon indicated, enormously technical, yet it was, and is, much more than that and has become extraordinarily important. The Federal Reserve Board, created in 1913, had surpassed the Bank of England as the world's most important central bank, chiefly because of the importance of the U.S. economy. Federal Reserve has a unique legal ability, which it performs in complex fashion. It creates new dollars. Like the public utilities that supply electricity, it supplies dollars to the domestic and world economies according to perceived needs. Who defines these perceived needs? The Fed alone. But it does not manufacture these needs. The economy does. A public utility, for example, builds more lines, electrical substations, and transformers when new homes, office buildings, and shopping centers go up. As electricity is a vital commodity necessary to keep all these enterprises going, so is money vital as the essential power for a growing economy. Too little of it, and the economy powers down. But here the analogy breaks down. A public utility can keep track of the demand for electricity quite easily. A central bank cannot easily gauge the demand for money that will cause an economy to operate at maximum efficiency. Too many dollars stunt the very growth process the central bank is trying to nurture. Instead of new jobs, new businesses, new investments, a surplus of new dollars merely causes higher and higher prices.

Running monetary policy is as much an art as it is a science. One has to be both a good technician and a good "artist" to do it right. It requires an understanding of the dynamic relationships in the economy, both domestically and internationally, and a certain feel for what financial markets are thinking, or are apt to think. The Fed is constantly trying to anticipate markets. But it has a real problem. Monetary policy is inherently slow in its impact on the real economy. An analogy would be if you applied your car's brakes and it didn't stop for at least six months. But what if the economy is already slowing down when the brakes are applied? That could cause an unintended recession. These lags give the job that artistic flavor. Knowing when to move is as important as how to move.

Volcker fancied himself as good an artist and scientist of monetary policy as there was around. As president of the New York Fed, he sat as a permanent member of the policymaking Federal Open Market Committee (FOMC), where he often pressed for tighter money in the Carter years. Since the early 1950s, he had worked with or around monetary policy in one way or another, and he knew its limitations.

At another point in American economic history, Volcker might never have been considered for the Fed chairman post. Technicians, no matter how talented, rarely rise to such heights when they must rely on the judgment of politicians to elevate them. Jimmy Carter's first instinct was to seek a big, well-recognized name like Rockefeller or Clausen, and although Volcker was Carter's reluctant, and perhaps third, choice for the key post, it turned out to be the best appointment the Georgian ever made in his four years in the White House. Though there were many occasions in 1980, when interest rates began soaring as a result of Volcker's policies, that Carter regretted his decision, there was very little he could do about it, and most financial and political leaders agree that Volcker turned out to be the artist the economy so desperately needed.

STRANGE EVENTFUL HISTORY

The naming of Volcker as Fed chairman was in many respects a historical accident. It came about only because two points in history converged.

One, the banking system realized it was in deep

trouble, with inflation raging throughout the world. Credit itself had become a joke, a one-way deal that favored the borrower, who could take out a loan, get a tax deduction for the interest, and pay back in cheaper dollars. Banks were actually receiving negative interest on their loans, meaning that, after discounting for inflation, they were losing. Financial institutions felt that a house of cards was being built that would soon collapse. They began to realize that it was time to apply tough medicine, and one of the strongest, most effective candidates they could imagine for this task was Paul Volcker.

The New York Times once described Volcker as one of a breed of eastern money men who have run U.S. economic and financial policy since Alexander Hamilton and the founding of the republic. To be sure, Volcker springs from that tradition, but he differs in many ways, too. For one thing, he is not a wealthy man, although he could have long ago abandoned public service and made millions. Second, Volcker doesn't consider himself one of the boys of an exclusive club and holds in contempt many of the bankers who have so vigorously pushed his name to the fore. He believes that many of them are inept and greedy and made bad loans in the 1970s when they should have known better.

Why, then did the financial institutions like him? Because he played the right music for their ears. He supported the preservation of financial assets, which were under threat because of a roaring inflation. The lack of confidence of financial instutions in the economic policies of the Carter administration forced a crisis that brought Volcker on the scene. In a real sense, this marked a change in the emphasis of economic policy. It moved away from the "real economy," where goods and services are produced, to the "paper economy," the financial assets that undergird the real economy.

The second historical point pushing Volcker to center stage was the death of Keynesianism as the intellectual driving force in American economics. *Keynesianism* be-

came the generic name for the type of post–World War II
economic policies that emphasized maximizing employment and held that recessions could be avoided or minimized through manipulation of the federal budget.

A thumbnail sketch of Keynesianism goes like this:
The government would run a deficit when the economy
slows to feed more purchasing power into people's pockets;
it would run a surplus in inflationary boom times, perhaps
by raising taxes or cutting spending, to remove some of
this purchasing power and slow down overheated business
activity. With a little less money in the economy, prices
would not be bid up by people seeking more goods and
services.

But politicians soon found they were not good manip-
ulators and, indeed, could not muster the political will or
support for budget surpluses when they were needed. This
was a key failure of Lyndon Johnson's administration—his
decision to push for both guns and butter. As inflation
began to coexist with high unemployment, the theory—or,
more accurately, the distorted practice of the theory by
U.S. presidents and Congress—came under increased fire.
Yet Carter proved to be one of its biggest practitioners,
pressing policies to drive down employment shortly after
taking office in 1977. The administration actively tried to
reduce the value of the dollar and succeeded. Easy money
flowed from Miller's Federal Reserve shop. Inflationary
forces began to build. Because the price of oil was denom-
inated in dollars, the dollar's steep decline hurt OPEC's
revenues, causing the oil producers to boost prices in 1979,
scaling the fate of Keynesianism in American economics.

Volcker never bought many of the central ideas of
Keynesianism—that a little inflation was all right in the
interest of taking the edges off the business cycle. He
thought the followers of Keynes had turned his ideas into
a simplistic theory of economic fine-tuning, in which a
little inflation was tolerated in order to create more jobs.
To him, it was, as he put it, "bullshit."

All these years of Keynesianism added up to a mid-

1979 economic crisis, with inflation the main culprit. It was roaring along at an annual rate of 13.2 percent when Volcker took office. Carter went to the annual economic summit conference in Tokyo in June and received the bad news there that OPEC had decided to virtually double the price of oil, which meant more inflation and less economic output in the U.S. In addition, gasoline lines were reappearing in the U.S., the result chiefly of the government's own faulty allocation regulations. More ominous was the fact that confidence in the dollar was dropping rapidly. People were abandoning "paper" assets like bonds and bank certificates and investing in gold, jewelry, and other tangibles. It seemed the nation was on the verge of collapse as the value of the dollar plummeted, with all the negative economic and political ramifications that follow. Any strong and ambitious foreign policy decisions were thinly veiled because of the weak, volatile currency, as Carter finally discovered.

Vice President Mondale was the point man in Volcker's selection. "What happened was that with the soaring oil prices and the consequent drop in the value of the dollar and the inflation and so on, we had gotten to the point that the bond market was demoralized," Mondale said. "Management of our monetary affairs just was no longer seen as credible by many in the financial community. It was an intolerable situation that had to be corrected. When Blumenthal left, we were really in a crisis because our central team was gone. We had to move Miller to Treasury immediately to get that under control. We had to appoint somebody of unquestioned and immediate authority and legitimacy, including a reputation for independence and toughness to reassure the financial markets, to buy back legitimacy and reassure our major trading partners and our partners in the international financial institutions. We had to move fast. I knew Volcker from my Senate days and felt pretty sure that he would fit what we needed. But the president also wanted to look around at others. I think that at all times Volcker was a very strong candidate because of the severe and disastrous situation in which we found ourselves in the economic picture. You can't run a country with a demoralized bond market. It was one of the imperatives that had to be dealt with. [Former Fed chairman Arthur F.] Burns had some of that authority. We had to get it back and get it back fast."

SAVIOR OR GADFLY

This born-again president needed an economic savior. Quite by chance, he found him in Paul Volcker. But he did not particularly care for the scripture that Volcker laid out, with the sacrifices it would ask of Americans and of the president himself when the next election rolled around. Yet, as his press secretary, Jody Powell, noted, Carter could not at that point even think about the 1980 election, so palpable and intense was the crisis of the moment.

On July 25, 1979, Carter held a press conference and announced Volcker's nomination as chairman of the Federal Reserve Board. Two weeks later, on August 6, 1979, he administered the oath of office to Volcker and said, "Now is no time to change course." This statement indicated that the president felt the mere appointment of Volcker would calm the raging storm in the markets and that his present policies, given time, would work.

But financial markets do not place much faith in symbolism, and, besides, Volcker was more than just a totem for the Carter administration. When Carter interviewed him, Volcker laid it out straight. He said he would tend to run a tighter monetary policy than Miller and would insist on independence from politics for the central bank. Carter at the time obviously didn't know how tight he meant or how insulated from the political process Volcker would become, or he might have passed up Volcker. Soon Carter was to find out what this appointment really meant. At his swearing-in ceremony, Volcker gave some indication that he might try something innovative to cure the inflation. "We are face to face with economic difficulties really unique in our experience," he said, "and we have lost that euphoria that we had 15 years ago, that we knew all the answers to managing the economy."

A variety of answers had been tried since the relative price stability of the 1960s disappeared in the 1970s. President Nixon slapped on wage-price controls in 1971, a system that lasted for three years before it was abandoned in disgrace. President Ford tried "jawboning" business and labor leaders to hold their wages and prices down. Carter came back with voluntary wage-price guidelines to try to keep inflation in check. But the basic problem was that the U.S. government was incapable of keeping the budget under control. Demands by people for more services and for more tax reduction built enormous pressure on the budget, so much so that the deficit mushroomed to gigantic proportions in the 1980s, reaching $220 billion in fiscal 1986.

The public was not prepared for what was about to come. The economy had entered a slowdown in 1979, even with raging inflation, and expanded by only 2.8 percent that year, which was recession-type growth. When Volcker took office, the unemployment rate rose slightly to 5.7 percent, and the general public impression was that Volcker would follow a cautious, steady policy. As a *New York Times* editorial put it a day after his appointment:

. . . The Fed isn't likely to make any sudden shifts. Mr. Volcker, after all, helped formulate the world's current cautious, pragmatic stance toward the economy, and he no doubt shares the mood of its members. They rightly fear the potential damage of committing the board to a monetary attack on either inflation or unemployment before the severity of current recession is better understood. If there are changes, the changes will be largely symbolic. Mr. Volcker is widely viewed as a defender of a strong dollar. He is not, in fact, likely to find it much easier

than his predecessor to reconcile that goal with domestic economic growth. But the confidence that the
international banking world evidently places in the
chairman-designate should help.

Two months from the day of taking office, on October
6, 1979, Volcker revolutionized monetary policy, persuading his colleagues at the Fed to change the way it had been
operating for years. Rather than trying to control the
precise level of interest rates, the central bank would focus
on keeping the money supply under control. Interest rates
would, for the most part, be free to seek their own level,
meaning that they could go as high as the markets would
permit.

This was not caution, but boldness with a capital B.
The new chairman was attacking inflation straight on with
the toughest, clumsiest, bluntest economic tool known in
modern times—tight money—and it led to the deepest
recession since the 1930s. He did it with courage, and he
did it with political skills that mere technicians aren't
supposed to possess.

With the help of his supporting cast at the Federal
Reserve, he literally halted the public's expectations that
inflation would continue rising at double-digit annual
rates. Expectations of higher inflation are critical to its
continuing. They also affect what interest rates are charged
on longer-term assets such as mortgages and bonds. If
people don't think inflation is under control, interest rates
will be higher.

He miscalculated more than once along the way, and,
in the minds of many of his critics, he pursued his tight
monetary policies with an unnecessary harshness and utter
disdain for the lives of ordinary Americans who suffered
under the yoke of tight money. To Volcker, the inflation
fight was the only way to proceed, and, in its own way, it
was a profoundly moral course, in that it saved the nation
from the self-destructive power of inflation.

The Carter administration, though it saw a need for

higher interest rates to settle down the financial markets, was extremely worried about the new Federal Reserve policy of focusing entirely on the money supply. It tried without success to talk Volcker out of it before the Fed formally launched its program.

THE WAR YEARS: AN UNEASY VICTORY

The Volcker era, from 1979 to 1982, is one of the most significant in modern American economic history, a turning point so sharp that many who had invested their faith—and their earnings—in the belief that inflation would remain high forever found their assets suddenly less valuable. Volcker's appointment and subsequent actions moved the United States away from the very real threat of Banana Republic inflation and created the conditions for noninflationary growth. Carter's reelection chances were severely damaged, but President Reagan owes a good part of his 1984 reelection to Volcker.

After Volcker's policies conquered inflation, the economy came roaring back in 1984. Unemployment began to fall and inflation remained low. Reagan got the political credit for seemingly putting the economy aright.

Volcker's actions clamped down on the manufacturing sector, where Carter drew much of his support, and weakened the president's popularity, as well as his credibility as an economic manager. It was hard to explain that the Fed chairman he had named was making his own constituencies suffer.

After all the tough-medicine, Volcker could claim only partial success. Because his policies were combined with massive budget deficits incurred in the Reagan administration, the economy was left sailing in dangerous and uncharted waters. With his tight monetary regime came new problems: the appearance of the Third World debt problem, a heavy reliance on foreign borrowing to keep alive America's consumption binge, and a deterioration in the nation's competitive edge in world markets. Assessing the situation, Volcker puts it simply: "I think we're still pretty vulnerable."

For all his successes, the Fed chief could only tame the fires of inflation rather than extinguish them, and then only temporarily. He could do nothing to restore the nation's lagging productivity from which its real wealth is created, nor on his own reduce the massive budget deficit, the cause of many of the country's economic difficulties.

Many of his critics said he could have managed it better, something that's easy to say in hindsight. Their chief rap against Volcker is that he should have spread the tight money over five or six years, gradually squeezing it out of the system. By doing it so swiftly, they said, he severely damaged some of the underpinnings of the economy and unnecessarily caused more bankruptcies. They point to Japan as a country that did a much better job of managing the era from high to low inflation. But this isn't Japan; it's the U.S., with entirely different traditions and methods of operations. It's also the predominant world economy and possesses the world's chief currency. When a crisis occurs in the international financial system, people do not look to Tokyo to solve it. They look to Washington, especially to the marble palace at the intersection of 20th Street and Constitution Avenue, N.W., known as the Federal Reserve Board.

A more serious problem flows from Volcker's years at the Fed—the cult of personality that has grown up around him. During his term in office, the Fed abandoned its operating procedures that guide how much money should be created for a growing economy, because they didn't work anymore. Since no hard-and-fast formula exists, the central bankers have been reduced to relying heavily on their own judgment. Thus, the nation's financial markets have placed enormous faith in Volcker's judgment to do the right thing.

"If you have to have a system run on pure discretion— which is what we have—then I would vote for Volcker to run it," supply-side economist Jude Wanniski told *News-*

week magazine in 1986. "I wouldn't want anyone else running the Volcker standard other than Volcker." This presents long-term problems for the operation of monetary policy. While many talented people are around with the ability to run the nation's central bank, few have the background and the reputation of a Volcker. Financial markets seek out stability and rally around those with proven track records, something that takes a long time to build.

Volcker's war on inflation, with all its twists and turns and doubts and fears, embellished an already considerable legend. The fight was not pretty or smooth. But he managed to do one thing where others had failed in the past: he stuck with it.

2
TALL PAUL

Things always seemed to happen when Paul Volcker went on fishing trips. Big things.

One summer he and friends Gerald Corrigan and Ed Yeo went to a peaceful lake in an isolated part of Montana. Corrigan at the time was president of the Minneapolis Federal Reserve Bank and was soon to become head of the New York Fed, and Yeo was a Fed advisor.

They were enjoying the lake, the atmosphere, and the fishing when someone in a boat paddled up. "The Argentina ambassador is on the telephone," he said. Volcker, ever the good negotiator, told the man to tell the ambassador he would call him back.

They finished their fishing and drove into the small town nearby, a mere crossroads, in search of a telephone. The only outside telephone booth was occupied by two cowboys who had passed out from too much drink. So the second most powerful man in Washington and his companions walked into the Old Saloon to find a telephone. It was not all that crowded, and there was one soused barfly nursing his drink. They didn't pay much attention to the strangers. Volcker asked the bartender if he could use the telephone. He called the White House switchboard, and, when the operator couldn't find the ambassador immediately, he gave her the number of the saloon and told her to ask for "Mr. Jones" when she finally reached the ambassador.

Soon the phone rang. "Mr. Jones," the bartender said, sensing that somehow Volcker was Mr. Jones. Volcker's resonant voice could be heard throughout the bar. As he became more intense in the conversation, he grew louder. At one point, he said, "Five billion dollars! Do you realize how much five billion dollars is, Mr. Ambassador?"

Volcker looked around. Everyone in the saloon was looking at him, including a once oblivious, but now highly alert, barfly. He had gotten their attention.

Volcker has a way of getting people's attention. When President Reagan was considering whether to appoint Volcker to a second term in 1983, a top official in the Federal Reserve system said he had no doubt about the outcome. "If it isn't Volcker, there will be seismic waves throughout the whole international financial system," he said. Then, with a slight tinge of jealousy, he paused to consider what made Volcker such a shoo-in. "What is it about him? Why does he seem to have that magic? Is it that six-foot-seven-inch frame, or the suits he gets from Good Will, or the drugstore cigars? What is it, anyway?"

That "magic" is all these things and more. Barber Conable, president of the World Bank, detected it as early as 1969 when, as a congressman from New York, he attended a conference in London of U.S. congressmen and British parliamentarians. "Paul at the time was undersecretary of the Treasury for monetary affairs in the Nixon administration. Whenever Paul opened his mouth, the whole room fell silent. Everybody wanted to listen to Paul Volcker. He was already a commanding presence in international dialogue. I met him before but had very little contact with him. I came away from the conference thinking, boy, this is a personage."

That aura partly reflects the key economic positions he's held in his career. People have a tendency to respect and listen to people in power. But if that were all it is, Volcker would be no different from any other staff person who's held key positions in government. Volcker's strength emanates from a combination of skills. He has a quick, expansive intellect, which he uses diligently to obtain information about the economy. He has a strong sense about markets and where they are headed. He was not afraid to act when he felt the time called for it, even if the timing did not suit political leaders. But he is also a good politician in his own right, developing his own network of supporters in Washington and around the world. Despite some slippages along the way, especially in his acquiescence to 1980 credit controls, he has kept intact a reputation for integrity.

A SIXTH SENSE FOR CRISIS MANAGEMENT

The chief reason for Volcker's magic was that he showed himself to be a superb crisis manager in a world economy that has bounced from crisis to crisis in the last quarter-century. It has been the era of crisis managers, and the best ones always rise to the top. "He learned from every experience," said Robert Roosa, a former top Treasury Department official who was Volcker's mentor. "He was made literally aware of his special aptitudes and qualifications for handling these episodes." Fresh out of college and under Roosa's tutelage, young Volcker handled a few mini-crises as a specialist in trading government securities at the Federal Reserve Bank of New York in the 1950s. Then, as an aide to Roosa in the Treasury Department in 1963, he helped take actions to defend the dollar and close down banks when President Kennedy was assassinated. The dollar crisis of the early 1970s and the inflation crisis of the 1980s secured his reputation.

Accumulated experience certainly enhanced Volcker's self-confidence in dealing with the financial problems that flared up during his public tenure. But there was something else, too, something akin to a sixth sense. "He had very little faith in economic forecasts and no faith at all in econometric models," said Richard Syron, who was his special assistant in 1981 and part of 1982. "He's highly analytical, and he has an intuitive feel for markets. Whenever Volcker went on the road and called in, his first question was 'What's going on in the markets?'"

More than any Federal Reserve chairman in modern times, Volcker played an active, day-to-day role in the Fed's chief function, the buying and selling of government securities to influence the money supply, and thus the U.S. economy. This job is performed by the Federal Reserve Bank of New York, which has to operate within the general economic guidelines laid out every six weeks or so by the FOMC (Federal Open Market Committee), which included Volcker, the 6 other board governors, and 5 of the 12 regional Federal Reserve Bank presidents. (There is a rotation system for Fed bank presidents to sit on the FOMC.) When Volcker took over as chairman, the people who ran the New York trading desk in government securities found him questioning and often overruling their recommendations on how much in the way of government securities to buy or sell that day. There is nothing improper in this, of course, but the degree to which Volcker did it contrasted sharply with former chairmen.

Volcker, though, was halfway repentant about his hands-on style. "I've probably got a few people around here intimidated," he said. "I probably do it a little too much." But anyone who knows Volcker knows that he couldn't help himself. Many who thought they had as good a feel for the markets as Volcker resented his interference, but they could do nothing about it. Some interpreted it as arrogance, but others saw it as Volcker's own supreme self-confidence in his ability to assess the markets and make a decision. In many respects, he was a one-man central bank. "His wife was once quoted as saying that 'Paul believes that no one else in the world can do the job he's doing,' and that's basically true," said one former Fed official. Volcker, for that reason, did not delegate authority well, except to a few close allies, like Corrigan.

One Fed official said that Volcker was so sure of his ability to run monetary policy that, when he wanted to bounce his ideas off someone else, he'd pull the closest person around into his office so he could give his spiel, even if that person happened to be the cleaning lady.

Like all quick impressions people form of others, this one is an exaggeration. Actually, Volcker is an agonizer, one who invited staff members to question his decisions or ideas in order to make sure that every avenue had been taken into account. "He wanted to make sure that everything had been thought through, that no other consideration had been ignored," said one former staff member. "He would call you in and say, 'Here's the decision. What do you think?' He would argue with you if you made a statement about it. 'What support do you have for that statement?' If you didn't he'd say, 'You'd better find support if you want to make that argument.'"

Many staff members found this extremely intimidating, but it forced them to arm their opinions with facts and avoid mental sloppiness. The sounding-board approach proved to be a useful antidote for his hierarchical manner. It injected a note of caution into his decisions, even though he didn't always follow the advice he received.

There was more than just personal operating style involved. Monetary policy was such a harsh instrument that it could have many unintended side effects, and the chairman often worried about them.

When his tight money really began to take hold and interest rates rose to record levels, Volcker agonized over whether his policy was going to cause permanent damage to the economy. Throughout much of the 1970s, the productivity, or efficiency, of the U.S. economy had begun to sag. The future health of any economy—its jobs, profits, wealth, and well-being—relies crucially on how productive it is. To Volcker, greater investment was the answer to higher productivity, and higher interest rates added to the cost of financing this investment. If he dropped interest rates, however, there would be no effective weapon against inflation, which would wreck the economy, too.

Volcker's mind probes deeply into a subject, any subject. Richard Syron recalled a penetrating conversation when they took a short walk from the Fed's offices at 20th and Constitution in Washington just down the street to the State Department. Volcker began asking him about automobiles, a subject that Syron knew a lot about because he had almost become an automotive engineer. The conversation went something like this:

Volcker: What's the advantage of front-wheel drive?

Syron: It is more efficient to have the wheels pulling rather than pushing the car. The wheel under power has more traction.

Volcker: Why is that more economical?

Syron: The car weighs less. The transmission is integrated.

Volcker: Why is the hump still there on front-wheel drives?

Syron: It's needed for the strength of the unibody, or the chassis.

Volcker: How much will 200 to 300 pounds less in weight contribute to fuel economy? How much will that save a consumer and save the economy if everyone had a front-wheel drive?

Both men talked about rough monetary calculations in their heads to answer Volcker's question as they walked into the State Department. Syron found this exchange not at all unusual and, in fact, typical of Volcker's probing mind. "It grasps on to something with steel claws," he said.

Even at Thanksgiving dinners, relatives and friends invited over find Volcker playing this game with them. His son Jim said that, as different points of view begin to emerge from various parts of the table, his dad takes over and starts orchestrating the conversation in an effort to drive it to some conclusion. "He'll say, 'You've had your say; let someone else speak,' or 'Have you thought of this?' " Thanksgiving dinners at the Volcker house sometimes resemble meetings of the Federal Open Market Committee.

In a delicate and sensitive way, he used this method to help Jim gain some badly needed self-confidence. At the time, Volcker was still president of the Federal Reserve Bank of New York, and Jim had decided to take some graduate courses in economics at New York University. "He helped me with the course. He would answer a question with a question. I think it's a good way to learn. We would spend hours on a Sunday afternoon or a Saturday afternoon. It wasn't just the first answers you'd go after. He'd ask a few other, deeper questions about the same theory to make sure I really understood what I was doing. He was really a big plus and a help at that point. I got to enjoy the subject matter and understand it based on our subjects. Based on that, I decided to major in the subject."

In addition to helping his son understand, it provided therapy and brought the two closer together. Through it all, Jim could never discern what economic philosophy his father personally favored. "One thing about my dad is that he loves a good argument as long as you can back your side of the story up. He's very open-minded. Even today, I'm not quite sure what his real bent is. My feeling is that he's a pragmatist and consensus-builder. I guess you have to be in that job."

To this day, daughter Janice remembers those arguments. "I won only one argument with him in all the time I was growing up, and it was over the spelling of a word," she said. "I don't remember the word, only that I won. He was always right over everything."

THE HALLMARKS OF A FORMIDABLE OPPONENT

Volcker could be tough when challenged. He once threatened the Treasury that he would go public with a complaint if it did not back down on some outrageous statement it had made about the currency markets. The Treasury backed down quickly and apologized. Although few have seen it in public, Volcker can get angry—an intense, icy kind of anger that knows it is right and usually is. Former Treasury Secretary Donald T. Regan at times was the target of this anger. Volcker also knew how to twit Regan in public, as he once did in a meeting of the Depository Institutions Deregulation Committee, which was in the process of removing regulations from interest rates that institutions paid depositors. Regan was arguing for a different interest rate limit than Volcker, but Volcker pointed out publicly that, if Regan's rate were compounded, it amounted to the same rate that Volcker was proposing. This embarrassed Regan, an old Wall Streeter proud of his financial prowess, enormously.

Volcker was also one of Washington's best infighters. When the White House assigned Vice President George Bush to head a task force on designing legislation to combine all the banking regulators into one super-regulator, Volcker managed to fight it off. William Isaac, chairman of the FDIC (Federal Deposit Insurance Corporation), had visions of becoming that top regulator. Before it was over, though, regulatory power in Washington was carved up. Half went to the Fed, and the other half went to the Treasury, under Donald T. Regan. The FDIC actually lost some of its power, and the idea of a super-regulator went down the drain.

Around the family especially, Volcker also displays an almost comic competitive nature. Robert Kavesh, a friend and a professor at New York University, called Volcker one of the best Monopoly players he had ever seen and said the Fed chief delighted in winning, never showing any mercy. "You'd think your father would let you win one once in a while," said Janice.

Kavesh countered with a table hockey game and beat Volcker mercilessly. The Fed chairman then bought his own game and practiced for the next match. "When he thought he was ready, he called me up to come over and play," Kavesh said. "I still clobbered him."

As for the pragmatism Jimmy sees in his father, it is often forgotten that it is an important requisite of power. Ideologues establish boundaries around themselves that make them predictable and highly suspect. If Volcker had been identified publicly as being rigidly of one persuasion or another, he would have lost some of his effectiveness. One of the Fed's chief weapons in the financial markets is the element of surprise, and a strong element of pragmatism is required in order to produce these surprises from time to time.

Volcker showed that he knew where he wanted to take monetary policy over the long run, said a former Fed official, and that was to push for noninflationary growth, with emphasis on the adjective and not the noun. He strayed from the target in only small ways, compromising to maintain his power as well as he could, he said.

It is only fitting that Volcker was chairman of the Federal Reserve. Jim said that he has so many layers of reserve that, in order to discover his real emotions, "I have to peel him." Volcker's wife Barbara once asked him when he came home from work what kind of day he had had, and he responded, "You have to understand that, when you ask me a question like that, my mind just closes."

Volcker's aloof manner masks an animated personality who loves a good time with close friends, preferably with sparkling conversation. He is extremely selective in forming friendships, choosing those with similar intellect, interests, and viewpoints. Once he went to a costume party dressed as the Jolly Green Giant and was the life of the party. He loves banter, and his idea of a joke is often pulling someone's leg. His personal warmth can be extensive, but it does not extend too far beyond a close circle of friends. First-time acquaintances, or those who have a casual relationship with him at work, often find him cold and sometimes impenetrable.

He guards his inner thoughts as he guarded a secret about when he would change the Fed's discount rate.

Volcker does not get close to many people, even within his own family. But his family members all say that he got closer to sister Louise than anyone, perhaps because she and Paul shared a quick wit and facility for banter. She came to visit his family often when he was working for Chase Manhattan and she was a social worker. Rarely have members of his family seen Volcker with tears in his eyes. He cried when Louise died of cancer in 1967 at age 46.

CHAMPIONING THE VIRTUES OF OLD

As chairman of the Fed, Volcker lived near his offices in an apartment cluttered with newspapers, cigar butts, and fishing flies that he had tied himself. He bought a washer and dryer for his daughter Janice, a nurse in northern Virginia, and then proceeded to carry over his laundry every week or so in a suitcase. "I could see I was getting corralled into that," said Janice. Volcker lives austerely and hates to spend money, unlike the bankers he regulates. "He'll spend money to go out to dinner, but he's cheap on other things, like his clothes are kind of rumpled up," Janice said. "He really doesn't care a lot about his appearance. He's just sort of cheap. I remember we had this old car when we were living in Plainfield [N.J.], and it was this old green Ford. That car was just falling apart. I remember at one point the front seat fell back. He took the kitchen stool and propped up the back of the seat for a couple of years. He just didn't want to go buy a new car."

At the time, Volcker was a high-level executive of Chase Manhattan Bank.

Volcker is cheap about restaurant prices, too. Once when Jude Wanniski, one of the gurus of the supply-side economics movement, took him to dinner at the Four Seasons Hotel in Washington's posh Georgetown section, Volcker used the occasion to needle Wanniski, saying "What are we doing in such a swanky place? Look at those prices! I have to go back to the office and tighten." Robert Kavesh said Volcker is serious in his complaints about high prices when he goes out to eat.

Kavesh, in fact, calls Volcker a Miniver Cheevy, after the fictional Edwin Arlington Robinson character who longed for the days of yore. He does seem to have a puritanical streak in him that yearns for the days when banks made sounder loans and when dedication to the public service was a widely accepted virtue.

"He's very old-fashioned," said Janice. "He'd probably like to see all women in dresses, including his daughter."

As important to Volcker as frugality is self-sufficiency, which he has stressed with his children. When he moved from Washington to New York in 1975, Jim, then a teenager struggling with his cerebral palsy, came up to him and said, "Dad, I think it's time we checked out this subway system." His father told him that, if he wanted to check out the subway system, that was all right with him and sent him out alone. Young Jim was concerned, but he made it all right and came back with a greater sense of confidence.

Neither would Volcker dispense economic advice to Janice or her husband, who is in the pension field. While Volcker was squeezing tightly on the money supply in 1981 to control inflation, he declined to give his daughter and son-in-law advice when they were trying to buy a home in the midst of soaring mortgage rates. They finally wound up paying 15 percent interest.

"He would never ask a favor of anybody else," said Janice.

Volcker's son went through numerous operations when he was a boy. When Jim was four years old and still had not walked, his father promised to buy him a Superman suit if he would walk across the foyer. "I wanted that Superman suit more than anything else," Jim said, so he walked for the first time. Later, his father rigged up a special table so that Jim could stand and swing at softballs, which Volcker tossed to him endlessly. When he hit one, Janice would run the bases for him.

This touching picture of Volcker isn't often painted because he was so much involved in the pressure of his job, but the facade of tough, intimidating, cold central banker is misleading. Those who have worked for him call him one of the most complicated men they have ever met.

Does Paul Volcker have a heart? Yes, he does, according to his family. But those who suffered through the worst spell of unemployment since the Great Depression in 1981–82 thought differently. So did those who had borrowed to beat inflation, only to find themselves the losers because of falling prices.

Volcker's family and friends said the economic suffering pained him. "Publicly, he was seen as being cold, theoretical, and insensitive to all the suffering," said vice chairman Fred Schultz. "The truth of the situation is that Paul was sensitive to what was going on in the real world. He watched the markets very carefully. He talked to cab drivers. He was more sympathetic to the little guy than most people thought. We used to talk a lot about how people were getting hurt (by his policies). He would say, 'What are your alternatives? This is very bad that a lot of people are getting hurt, but the alternative is worse.' "

3
THE SATURDAY NIGHT SPECIAL

The inflation crisis of 1979 was to change many lives, but few as dramatically as Volcker's. As the 51-year-old president of the Federal Reserve Bank of New York, he had acquired an apartment on East 79th Street a few years earlier when the city was embroiled in financial crisis and housing was relatively cheap. On a $116,000 salary (not bad for the time), he managed to live comfortably with Barbara and Jimmy, then 21. Daughter Janice was married and living in Arlington, Virginia.

The White House's call for him to come and meet with Carter shattered that tranquility. It was not especially convenient for Volcker to give up his position in New York. Jimmy, a bright and highly personable man, was undergoing a difficult personal adjustment. At the time, he was coping with problems associated with the cerebral palsy that had affected his limbs since he was born. Here in New York, his father had grown closer to his son and was helping him to make the adjustments. "It wasn't an ideal time to be coming to Washington," he said.

Then his wife, who suffers from severe arthritis and diabetes, decided to stay in New York, both to be close to her doctors and to stay in the city she loved and knew well, where she could get around easily. Although he would call frequently and often commute home for weekends, the separation would still be difficult, and both Paul and Barbara knew it. Finally, because of the bizarre pay system in the federal government, in which the pay of top officials is linked to that of members of Congress, the chairman's job at the time paid only $57,000, which put a strain on the family budget despite a compensation package Paul received from the New York Fed. He would have to pay for housing in two separate cities, two of the most expensive in the world.

So, Volcker said, he was racked with ambivalence. He really didn't want to be named chairman of the Fed. He also knew something else: "If the president offered it to me, I knew I couldn't turn it down." It would be the pinnacle of his career and it would offer him a challenge the likes of which he had never had before, a chance for instant stardom and ego gratification—a difficult opportunity for anyone to turn aside.

The offer from Carter touched a deeper nerve. Back in Teaneck, New Jersey, a town of 35,000, Volcker had grown up as the son of the city manager, Paul A. Volcker, Sr., who had hammered into his children the duties and satisfactions of public service. Here, too, as a young man who had grown up during the Depression, he had heard his father, the son of a German immigrant, preach the merits of thrift and economic conservatism and how debt can be injurious.

A PRESCRIPTION FOR THE '80s: TIGHT MONEY AND AN INDEPENDENT FED

To Volcker, the 1979 climate offered only one clear answer, and he laid it out to Carter in his interview with the president: tighter money plus independence for the Fed.

According to Robert Kavesh, Volcker left with the distinct impression that he would not be appointed because of this blunt economic prescription. Volcker never knew about the infighting over his appointment, though he later found out that both Rockefeller and Clausen had been approached. His wife had also been told by the wife of Arthur Okun that the late economic advisor to President Johnson had been approached about the job by the White House.

As it turned out, Carter had *not* objected to his plan. When the call for the appointment came, it was confirmation from the president that more tightness was just the medicine needed.

Miller was not a hard act to follow. According to a number of people interviewed, he never exhibited great interest in the Federal Reserve and its complex tasks, and the financial markets rewarded him with a no-confidence vote. A former business executive at Textron, Miller damaged himself in the eyes of financial markets when he once dissented on a rise in the Federal Reserve's discount rate, the interest rate it charges banks for borrowings. The discount rate sets the pace for all other interest rates in the economy and, as such, provides a clue to the Fed's policies and attitude about the desirable level of interest rates. Miller also did not match the style of what the markets thought a prudent central banker should be. He was often making speeches in public or giving interviews to reporters on monetary policy. A former staff member recalls that Miller seemed more interested in his image than in Fed policy. Once, while he was driving to Capitol Hill to testify on monetary policy, Miller asked a staff member how his remarks would sound in the press, not how well thought out they were. He had fought efforts by the Carter Treasury months earlier to get the Fed to tighten monetary policy, one of the rare times in history the government in power has wanted tighter money than the monetary authorities.

Yet when Miller took over as Treasury chief, he stood next to Carter and Volcker and said that "inflation is a clear and present danger. It has struck at our nation's vitality. If it is not checked, it will threaten our democratic system itself." Despite these strong words, Miller in subsequent months found himself in disagreement with Volcker's tight-money policies to control inflation and frequently said so.

Volcker came in primed. As president of the New York Federal Reserve Board, he had a permanent seat on the FOMC, the policy-making arm of the Fed. Here he had seen the internal frustration of trying to bring a roaring inflation under control and the weaknesses of the Fed's operating system.

From a broader perspective, he was prepared to launch the central bank into an era of tight money that would bring inflation under control. This was an historic, highly ambitious goal, but he sensed that, at least at this point in time, the public and the political authorities were ready for it. How long they would remain supportive as the interest rates rose was certainly a big question in his mind and in the Fed's mind. From this point on, he and the Fed would become the focal point for economic policy. It meant that he must risk a recession and inflict a great deal of economic pain. How far could he push the American economy?

He knew, too, that he must act quickly and boldly. He had learned that lesson back in his earlier jobs at the Treasury Department, where he had engineered two dollar devaluations and even an end to the international monetary system that had existed since the end of World War II.

The practical effect of these actions was to unhinge the dollar from its fixed rate of exchange with other currencies, so that the dollar "floats" up and down in the markets. This led to today's much more volatile world financial system, with wider swings in the values of currencies and resulting financial uncertainty. Considering the alternative was a total breakdown of the world monetary system, there was probably no other practical choice.

THE ADVENT OF "PRACTICAL MONETARISM"

Volcker was primed from another standpoint. He knew that the Fed's operating system was simply not working very well in an era of high inflation. It was trying to do its job of supplying money and credit to the economy by using interest rates as a guidepost. Two things were wrong with this strategy. First, the Fed wasn't prescient enough to know how high interest rates would have to rise to control this raging inflation, nor would it be inclined to allow the rates to rise to such a level considering the political sensitivity of the time. Second, as Volcker put it, interest-rate targeting made the Fed too predictable. In an inflationary environment, the Fed would always loosen. When interest rates bumped up against the Fed's interest-rate target, everyone knew it was going to inject funds into the system to defend that rate. "It was like shooting fish in a barrel," Volcker said. But the injection of new money into the economy would quicken inflationary expectations, and that would drive up long-term interest rates (which react more to inflation fears than to Fed policy).

Volcker was ready to change this operating procedure almost from the time he took office. But how? He had been thinking about it a long time, in fact. In 1977, he had written a paper as president of the New York Fed supporting the idea that the Fed should keep within the monetary growth targets it was required to report each year to Congress under the Humphrey-Hawkins law. Doing this would not only communicate to the public the Fed's expectations of inflation, he wrote, but would serve as self-discipline within the Fed itself.

As noted by Fed analyst Donald F. Kettl, Volcker did not believe in using the money supply as the sole guide for policy. He favored an idea called "practical monetarism," which meant that the Fed ought to try to stay within its monetary guidelines but be quick enough to change policy if circumstances demanded. "It seems to me the essence of policy-making in these circumstances is that judgments must be made in the presence of uncertainty," Volcker wrote in a different paper in 1976.

Perhaps more than anything else, the new procedure would give the Fed political cover and insulation from political forces. It could say that it was not raising interest rates, just controlling the money supply.

Internally, Volcker had been intimately involved with Fed studies of making the switch from interest-rate targeting to money-supply targeting. In fact, it had been studied off and on for years. One of his predecessors, William McChesney Martin, had the idea studied but rejected it. Under Miller, the idea came under scrutiny again.

Volcker knew that doing away with the old focus on interest rates would be highly controversial, so he set out immediately to try to do a test run on switching to a system in which the Fed would use its monetary targets as a guide to how many new monetary reserves it added to the system. It meant that the staff people responsible for such things would keep two books, one showing how things worked under the current system and the other showing how they would work under a theoretical system. Computer printouts piled up on Volcker's desk, all appearing to show the plan would work. But he and his staff knew that the studies were nearly useless, because theoretical exercises couldn't predict how the financial markets, businesses, and ordinary people would react if such a system were really in effect.

Up to this point, the Fed had directed its activities at controlling interest rates, or the *price* of money. The new proposal suggested that that procedure had not worked. It was now time to emphasize controlling the *supply* of money and forget about the price for a time. Because of political restraints, you could never get the *price* high enough to restrain runaway inflation; besides, you might not even know what that price required to achieve that goal. On the other hand, technical work indicated that emphasizing controlling the *supply* of money would enable interest rates to rise high enough to curb inflation.

This was borrowing heavily from the monetarism preached by economist Milton Friedman, who believed that the Federal Reserve should let the money supply grow steadily and slowly, without regard to other factors occurring in the economy. But it was not totally Friedmanesque, because Volcker held out the necessity for some judgment. Friedman believed that judgment of human beings should not be a significant factor in monetary policy. While this difference of interpretation might seem small, it was gigantic.

SETTING A NEW COURSE: THE "HAWKS" VS. THE "DOVES"

Volcker's confirmation hearing before the Senate Banking Committee on July 30, 1979, established a persona that was to become familiar with the American public—an imposing man hunched over in his witness chair, puffing a cheap Antonio y Cleopatra drugstore cigar that emitted plumes of smoke around his bespectacled, balding head. These, and the rumpled suit or the tie that was often too short for his long trunk, became Volcker trademarks.

His confirmation went smoothly, as Volcker displayed his remarkable talent for dodging questions or seeming to answer them without hemming himself in. But the bulk of his answers that day left little doubt that he was going into the Federal Reserve with the full intention of being tighter. When Senator William Proxmire (D., Wisconsin), the committee chairman, asked him if he intended to raise interest rates to an even higher level, Volcker said he was only one member of the board with only one vote, a bit of a misleading answer since this was hardly reflective of his full powers as chairman of the board. But then he added, "I don't think there's any feeling or any evidence around at the moment that the economy is suffering grievously from a shortage of money."

In addition, he made it perfectly clear that he had little respect for the view of liberal economic policy that had dominated American life for most of the postwar period. When Proxmire quoted a study by Okun that tightening the money supply would exact a tremendous price from the economy in terms of lost production and jobs and would have little impact on inflation, Volcker was ready. Such studies didn't mean much, he said.

"And part of the difficulty—and part of what has helped to account for this—seems to me the fact that the prolonged nature of the inflation has changed expectations; it's changed the way people look at their personal lives and view the outlook for the economy, in an unfavorable way. . . . I think it's fair to say the economy probably doesn't react the way you and certainly I were brought up to think. In terms of economic analysis, we were taught that an expansionary dose by whatever technique would improve employment with maybe some risk of inflation. We proceeded on that assumption for a long time, and we found the risks of inflation became much greater and that reactions in terms of employment, output, and productivity got less. . . . I don't think we have any substitute for seeking an answer to our problems in the context of monetary discipline."

This man was going to be different, all right. After his confirmation, he set out to prove it. But in his first few weeks on the job, Volcker realized how difficult it was going to be—in convincing his own board and the financial markets that it was time for a new course.

Volcker found his board was split between the "hawks" and the "doves." The doves didn't like the idea of putting the economy "through the wringer," as they say, to squeeze out inflation. It would have, as Proxmire's question to Volcker implied, put too many people out of work and not even control inflation. The "doves" of Volcker's board were Charles Partee, Nancy Teeters, and Emmett Rice. The "hawks," on the other hand, believed there was no substitute for a sound dollar brought on by monetary

restraint. The "hawks" were Henry Wallich, Philip Cold-
well, and a brand-new appointment, Frederick Schultz, a
Florida banker and politician who later became a close
Volcker friend (much to the chagrin of some of Schultz's
buddies in the Carter administration). This was the way
they were perceived by the press, anyway, and to some
extent within the Fed itself. Teeters, Partee, and Rice,
though, proved to be solid hawks before it was over.

Volcker's first experience at being tighter was success-
ful as the board voted unanimously to raise the discount
rate from 10 to 10.5 percent. After that, it got much
tougher for Volcker. The board secretly voted down
another rise in the discount rate on August 31, and then,
on September 18, it split four to three to push up the
discount rate to 11 percent.

Volcker said a split vote was all right with him. As far
as he was concerned, four to three didn't matter as long as
he was winning. But financial markets interpreted that
vote as meaning that it would be the last time the central
bank could tighten, given the dynamics of voting within
the board. It did not make sense, but as many central
bankers have learned, they often have to react to irrational
thinking if that is what is driving the markets. The dollar
sank again, and this time the situation was more serious.

The Volcker rally and the Volcker honeymoon were
over. Something had to be done and done quickly. And
Volcker was marshalling his evidence internally to go to a
new system and break through this wall of incrementalism
that would send the Fed in an entirely different direction,
one that would bring it some credibility and at least give it
a chance to bring inflation under control. He began to
sound out the Fed members on the new proposal to target
the money supply.

Debate within the board on whether the plan would
work was intense. "We were groping," said one close to the
situation. "It became one big intellectual discussion.
Volcker himself did not try to do much persuading."

Volcker called his vice chairman, Schultz, into his

office around September 1 and asked him for his opinion on the new approach. "Paul, you know a great deal more about the effect of policy than I do," Schultz replied. "All I know is that it is apparent that we are going to have to do something. We need a major change that is going to affect psychology."

Robert Black, president of the Federal Reserve Bank at Richmond, said Volcker called him and told him that he was probably going to make such a proposal. Black, who has monetarist leanings and had dissented from the Fed's lackluster efforts to control inflation earlier in the year, didn't give Volcker a chance to ask for support. He said he was for it enthusiastically.

The reaction from the four to three discount rate increase, plus continuing turmoil in world financial markets, softened internal opposition. Partee, Teeters, and Rice were getting worried, too. The slide in the dollar could turn into a free-fall, and the last thing any central banker wants, even a fairly liberal one, is a currency that is declining rapidly in international markets. Partee and Teeters were highly skeptical of the new proposal, but in the final analysis they saw that the Fed had little choice but to use it to regain credibility.

Adhering to the targets would obviously mean tightening. For instance, for 1979, the Fed said it wanted the money supply to grow between 1.5 percent and 4.5 percent. In the third quarter, the money supply had surged by 9.5 percent, raising fears of renewed inflation. (The 1.5 to 4.5 percent figure was adjusted later to 3 to 6 percent for technical reasons.)

Volcker was eager to move his new proposal to final action, although he still wasn't certain he could sell it to the FOMC. One thing interfered as late September arrived, the annual meeting of the International Monetary Fund and World Bank. Although this was largely a ceremonial session, every finance minister and central banker who was anybody would be there, as would many private bankers and financiers. Volcker did not want to go, but his staff talked him into it. Making an appearance would give a measure of calm, while an absence might raise anxiety. The Fed chief relented, riding to the meeting in Belgrade, Yugoslavia, in a Treasury Department plane. Miller was aboard, and so was Charles Schultze, chairman of President Carter's Council of Economic Advisors.

Volcker knew he would need the administration's support, so he told both men in a general way what he had in mind. Both expressed reservations about the new approach in the discussions and began to try to talk Volcker out of it.

The trip, though, reinforced Volcker's determination to move. At a stopover in Bonn, West German officials, led by Finance Minister Helmut Schmidt, who later became the chancellor, gave Volcker an earful about the falling dollar and called for forceful action to bring the sitation under control. Although Volcker and Miller did not tip their hand, they received assurances from the West German government that it would not boost interest rates, too, if the U.S. took action to curb inflation by raising interest rates. This German attitude was welcome; it would offset the American effort to shore up the dollar.

In Belgrade, finance ministers and central bankers from around the world urged quick U.S. action. Volcker privately told an old friend, the late Otmar Emminger, formerly head of the West German central bank, of his idea of targeting the money supply and received support.

An impatient man when he is ready to act, Volcker was ready to leave Belgrade as soon as he arrived, but Schultze and Miller took him aside and told him that an early departure would create the wrong impression. The markets would think the U.S. was panicking. They managed to convince Volcker to stay one more day. The Fed chief thought that he could safely leave on Tuesday, so he slipped out of town. As soon as the financial people learned this, the story got out that Volcker was dashing home to scurry up some quick action to protect the dollar in view of all the bad things he had heard at Belgrade. His departure electrified the financial world.

The move did work to Volcker's advantage. Now all the world knew that a dollar-rescue plan was in the works. It was clear that, if something were not done by the following Monday, October 8, there would be a run on the dollar of massive proportions.

Once again, Volcker faced the Carter administration's top two economic advisors, Schultze and Miller, and once again they tried to talk him out of his planned action. They all met with Solomon in Miller's office. Schultze thought it meant a big recession, pure and simple, at some point in the future. "I thought he pulled a brilliant political move, but my argument was that once you tell the world that everything hinges on the money supply growth being kept unchanged and when you have to change it—and you know you are—you won't be able to do it. You will have locked yourself in. It turned out that he did lock himself in, but he managed to get himself out of it. What he gained by this was freedom to do what he had to—namely to get interest rates high enough to put the country through a big recession." Schultze and Miller argued that Volcker and the Fed should limit their action to raising the discount rate by a huge amount and not mess around with this new, and potentially dangerous, procedure.

According to Anthony Solomon, undersecretary of the Treasury for monetary affairs who organized this meeting, Volcker responded that a big discount rate change would bring another four to three split, which he contended would exacerbate the turmoil in financial markets. Solomon suggested a meeting with Carter so that Volcker could explain his plan, but it never came off. Instead, Miller later told Solomon that he had talked to the president about it and Carter had agreed that Volcker should not make the switch. Miller told Solomon to inform Volcker, but Solomon agreed with Volcker that he would be justified in making the change if the board were to split four to three once again on a discount-rate change, which would once again damage the Fed's credibility in the financial markets. Volcker thought that a discount rate change, while forceful, would not be enough to do the job and achieve the kind of credibility he wanted.

In fact, by this late hour, the split on the board began to subside with this deteriorating economic situation. Partee, for one, converted to the hawk side, seeing a need for dramatic action. The old policy of controlling interest rates was just not working, he said. Teeters said she had never considered herself either hawk or dove, despite how she was perceived publicly.

On Friday, October 5, word went out to the FOMC members to come to Washington for an emergency meeting. The board went to extraordinary lengths to hide the fact that the meeting was taking place, scattering the committee members in a number of hotels around the city. No one wanted the press to find out the FOMC was in town.

On the eve of the meeting, Volcker, Corrigan, and Fred Schultz went to dinner at one of Volcker's favorite restaurants, the Chez Camille. "We were worried about Paul," Schultz said. "He had been working very hard, and he was worried about the impact of going to this new feature." After a while, though, Volcker relaxed, and the three men were laughing, forgetting the pressures of the week. Just then Senator Alan Cranston (D., California) walked into the restaurant with a small party and recognized Volcker. Almost instantly, the merrymaking stopped. It occurred to all three that this may be putting on the wrong face considering the tough action that was to be taken on Saturday.

The FOMC met in a mood of high seriousness on Saturday, October 6. Volcker was not sure yet that he could pull it off. The reservations expressed by Charles Schultze were real. It did mean a long, tough period of tight money, and it would mean clamping down hard in the beginning. The economy wasn't that strong. It would put the Federal Reserve in an adversarial position not only with the White House, but also with many segments of the economy who had become accustomed to high inflation.

Pope John Paul II had just arrived in Washington for a meeting with President Carter and would deliver a Mass on the Washington Mall the following day. Some board members took note of this and wondered whether the pope was saying a prayer for what they were about to do.

A staff paper prepared by economists Steve Axilrod and Peter Sternlight said the new procedure would help the Fed bring the sharply rising money supply under control and help the central bank go into 1980 "money growth on a more moderate track than has prevailed recently. Announcement of such a shift in procedure may itself have a beneficial calming effect on inflationary psychology." The staff paper warned, however, that it was "not a simple, risk-free procedure that can quickly solve monetary policy problems."

Volcker played the role of devil's advocate, outlining the proposal and the chief objections and problems with it. He went around the room, giving everyone a chance to speak, as was customary with operations of the committee. "It was a masterful performance," said Fred Schultz. "By the time the meeting was over, he had the committee eating out of his hand."

Other Fed members recall that they had many questions about the viability of the proposal over the long haul. The minutes reflect that they certainly expected more fluctuations in interest rates and perhaps more economic volatility. None anticipated the actual problems that would develop with the system further down the road.

"There were a lot of questions about it," said one board member at the time. "It is not true that this was an easy meeting. It took practically all day, and we were not at all sure of how it would work."

At the end of the meeting, Volcker said, "It damn well

better work, or we'll have the same problem [high infla-
tion] all over again."

The board had decided to focus on the money supply
by keeping a specific limit on nonborrowed reserves it
provides to the banking system. Banks are required by the
Fed to keep a certain percentage of their deposits in
reserve. If the central bank creates new money, or reserves,
banks will have enough money to expand their lending. If
it tightens, or withdraws reserves from the banking system,
banks will be forced to scramble to find funds to meet
these reserve requirements. They most often do so by
borrowing from each other in overnight interbank lending
called the federal funds market. When the Fed does not
create enough money, the interest rate on this interbank
lending rises; when the Fed eases, reserves are easier for
banks to find and the rate falls.

The federal funds rate is the most critical short-term
interest rate in the economy. From it, all other short-term
interest rates are set, including the more prominent prime
lending rate or the government's Treasury bill rate. The
interest rates on many loans and savings accounts are
directly linked to the prime rate and the Treasury bill rate,
and that is directly related to Fed policy.

Prior to October 6, 1979, the Fed had tried to control
the federal funds rate directly as a way of keeping the lid on
inflation. Afterwards, it focused its attention on how many
reserves it was supplying to the banking system. Yet it still
kept a target for the federal funds rate, although the range
was wider than previously and the Fed would not try to
keep it rising higher if banks were forced by circumstances
to pay dearer rates because money was tighter.

The continued setting of this rate gave a real clue as to
where the Fed expected rates to go. The minutes of the
Fed's Saturday Night Special set the upper part of this
range at 15.5 percent. Teeters said this rate was set at the
time because no one, including Volcker, thought that

interest rates would rise any higher as a result of the momentous decision. When they dashed over this mark on their way to topping 20 percent, the Fed had no other choice but to lift the target for the federal funds rate higher to reflect reality.

Late in the evening of October 6, Volcker called in reporters to drop the financial bombshell. He began it with a sense of humor. "I will tell you that the major purpose of this press conference is to show you that I have not resigned—the way the early rumor had it yesterday. And I'm still alive—contrary to the latest rumor." He laid it out: the discount rate would jump a full percentage point from 11 to 12 percent. The Fed no longer would try to control interest rates directly, but would try to control the money supply within the annual growth targets it had already laid out. It required financial institutions to keep an extra 8 percent of their deposits on hand for their growth in large time deposits and dollar borrowings in Europe.

Although Volcker would later say that no one was deluded into thinking that the tough new policy would not ultimately lead to a recession, he was upbeat when it came to public consumption. Asked if it would slow down the economy, he said, "I would be optimistic about the results of these actions." Although he said economic events weren't fully predictable, ". . . just looking at recent history, expectations of the worst are not always a valid basis for policy-making. And I'm not inclined to sit here and say let's dream up the worst that can happen and base all our policy decisions on that kind of thought."

The new Fed chairman had surprised everyone, striking out in an entirely different direction. Milton Friedman expressed pleasure at the Fed's action but noted that it would take time to determine whether the central bank was truly monetarist. As events turned out, he was right to be skeptical. Liberal economists called it overkill and risky. Miller, who had tried to talk Volcker out of the procedure, made a speech warmly endorsing it. The White House, which wasn't especially happy about the decision, issued a statement of support shortly after the announcement.

The big news in the Sunday, October 7, newspapers was the pope's visit. The Fed's actions made page one news, too, but many of the articles were sketchy and did not capture the sweeping nature of the change.

The Volcker era had arrived in American economics and politics. It was to prove a profound transition for every household in America and throughout the world.

4
DER STAMMHALTER IST DA!

Paul A. Volcker, Jr., was born a central banker. He didn't know it at the time, of course, and never aspired to such a job until much later in life. "I didn't know the Federal Reserve existed when I was growing up," he said, discussing his youthful aspirations. Like many kids, he would perhaps have preferred playing professional baseball or basketball. Yet the family he was born into, and the values they imparted, prepared him well for the role of inflation-fighting central banker, which he was to assume in 1979.

Certain ideals were woven so intricately into his psyche during his growing-up years that nothing could unravel them later in life. Thrift. Orderliness. Caution. Dedication to the public trust. Disdain for ostentation and excessive consumption. Striving for stability. Strength and credibility. These qualities all good central bankers emulate and admire, but few have the wherewithal or the fortitude to carry them out.

Central bankers are a breed apart from the rest of

humanity. As the cliché goes, central bankers march to their own drummers and assume a financial policeman's role in society. They are aloof, secretive, frugal, independent, public-spirited, responsible, and judgmental. Though cautious, a good central banker senses when the right time has arrived to move to protect the currency and believes that it is part of the higher moral order to curtail excessive spending and borrowing by citizens.

Paul A. Volcker, Jr., picked up all of these qualities with ease, partly by instruction but mostly by osmosis as a young boy growing up in Teaneck, New Jersey. Teaneck seemed an unlikely place to garner some of these qualities, but it was ripe with them. What he hadn't been born with, young Volcker learned from his family and from his role as son of the city manager.

His towering family—a six-foot-four father, three sisters over six feet tall, and an intellectual mother (only five-foot-seven)—influenced him most directly. He inherited an aloof, cool manner from his father and a strong intellect from both of his parents.

It was no surprise to his family and friends who grew up with him in Teaneck that Paul A. Volcker, Jr., in 1979 had presumed to tackle the highest, and most stubborn, inflation of modern times with a ferocious single-mindedness. After all, it was his father who was hired as city manager of Teaneck only 49 years earlier to pull the city out of a financial crisis: $5 million in debt, as a matter of fact, big money in those days to a suburban community. And from the time he was a young boy, young Paul's friends and family sensed that he would one day do something important. "He had a star quality about him," said Alice Ingebretsen, then Johannsen, a neighbor of the Volcker's in Teaneck.

They called him "little Bud," or "Buddie," to distinguish him from his father, Paul Adolph Volcker, Sr., Teaneck's city manager and a civil engineer by training. Paul Sr. had moved to the three-story clapboard Dutch colonial home at 1301 Longfellow Avenue in 1930 from

Cape May, New Jersey, with his wife, Alma; three daughters, Ruth, Louise, and Virginia; and Paul Jr., the baby of the family. (There had been another daughter, Eleanor, who died four months after birth in 1922.)

Bud's birth in Cape May, on September 5, 1927, had a special significance in the family constellation. His grandfather, Adolph, a German immigrant, sent a telegram of joy to the new parents: "Der stammhalter ist da" (The standardbearer is here.). Adolph's three sons, Paul, Milton, and Harry, up to this point had produced girls. According to Bud's sister Virginia, there was a sense of "at last, a male has been born. There was nobody to carry on the Volcker name in the country until then. My grandfather, and my father, considered that to be very important, just as it was for Bud to have a son of his own later."

THE GERMAN INFLUENCE

Paul Jr. was born into a German family in which the dominant father figure, stereotypical as it may sound, was a living tradition. Young Bud respected his father. "*Stern* was not the right word to describe him," Paul Jr. said. "He was pretty austere and repressed. But he could be very funny. . . . My father was the big man in town. Everybody who was anybody knew him, and if I ever did anything wrong, they'd know who I was. When my friends went out knocking out streetlights, I stayed home. I couldn't risk getting picked up. I felt that pressure very strongly."

The German influence on his life came from both sides of the family. His grandfather, Adolph Volcker, was a German immigrant from near the Dutch border, a huge bulk of a man, six-foot-four and 300 pounds. "He was very autocratic," said Ruth. He was a tea and coffee salesman and met his future wife, Pauline Keyser, a school teacher in Hoboken, New Jersey, who had emigrated a few years earlier, in the new world. They were married in 1888 and moved to Brooklyn, and Paul Sr. was born in 1889.

Paul's mother, Alma Klippel, also was of German

descent, the daughter of Elias Klippel and his wife Bertha, immigrants who ran a dry goods store in Lyons, New York. Alma, an only child, was a graduate of Vassar and taught chemistry as a research assistant for a year before she went back to Lyons. There, Alma met Paul Sr., a civil engineer graduate from Rensselaer who was working on a project to rebuild the Erie Canal for the New York State Highway Department. They fell in love, and in 1915 they were married. A year later, their first child, Ruth, was born.

Grandpa Adolph never shed his accent or his stiff manner. With his handlebar mustache and his autocratic nature, it wasn't too difficult to guess his roots. Once, he was mistaken on the streets of New York as the captain of the *Bismarck*, creating a small, ugly scene before it was straightened out. German was often spoken around the house. "Whenever my grandparents didn't want us to know what they were saying, they always spoke in German," Ruth said.

Adolph began the Volcker tradition of fishing. He, Paul Sr., and Bud used to go on fishing trips to Maine during the summer, leaving the women behind to take care of the children. It became such a compulsion with Bud's father that neighbors often saw the city manager in the yard, casting a line in the grass to hone his skills. Why fishing in particular appealed to the Volcker clan isn't clear, but the Fed chairman took to it passionately in later life, taking along a few fishing buddies who also happened to work with him in the Federal Reserve System.

Paul and Alma Volcker settled in Lebanon, Pennsylvania, where he was a city engineer. Later, he moved to Cape May, New Jersey, where he was secretary of the Chamber of Commerce and then city manager. Then Teaneck, only four miles west of the George Washington Bridge, beckoned with its financial problems, and Paul Sr. responded.

The Depression was just beginning to settle in, and Teaneck (population 33,000) did not escape the hard times. Yet this suburban community of New York did not daily witness the severity of the economic downturn so evident on the streets of the city or the more depressed neighborhoods. Indeed, it had more of a small-town feeling to it than today's sprawling, nondescript suburbs, even though a large proportion of the population commuted by the West Shore Railroad to the downtown financial district and midtown Manhattan jobs. It was white, middle-class America, with a sprinkling of ethnic groups. "It was a very nice neighborhood," said Amanda Johannsen, the 91-year-old matriarch of the Norwegian family that lived on Longfellow Avenue. When Amanda turned 90 in July 1985, she received a note of congratulations from the chairman of the Federal Reserve Board, Bud Volcker.

MONEY DISCIPLINE—A LESSON LEARNED

Although many have speculated that Paul Jr.'s experience in living through the Depression may have had a big impact on his emphasis on economic stability later in life, he remembers the hardship mainly in a peripheral way. The family never wanted for food or drink or shelter, although it would help feed tramps who roamed the countryside in those days.

Paul's parents did, however, instill in him the discipline of frugality. According to Bud's sister Ruth, a retired research librarian, Paul Sr. never made much money, yet he managed to provide for his kids and send them through college. "I won't say he pinched pennies, but he watched money very closely," she said. "We were always considered lucky during the Depression because he had a job." The real penny-pincher in the family was actually Alma, who scraped and saved everything in sight, according to Virginia's daughter, Victoria.

In the hard times of the Depression, they allocated funds to their children sparingly. Ruth, for instance, went to Simmons College in Boston in the late 1930s and was given an allowance of $25 a month to take care of all her meals and transportation. It was rugged getting by on this allowance, forcing her to forgo the slightest luxury that other well-heeled classmates could enjoy without much thought. She rarely asked for money, but once she needed a new coat so badly she borrowed from her parents to pay for it. Dutifully, she said, "I paid them back."

When Paul started in Princeton a decade later, his allowance was the same—$25 a month. "He raised the roof about that," Ruth said. Yet his parents were loath to give in. It did not ring falsely when, years later, Volcker as chairman of the Federal Reserve Board would lecture Americans on living beyond their means and borrowing too heavily. It stemmed from genuine feeling and experience dating back to that $25.

"He learned central banking on $25," said sister Ruth.

Paul was right to protest. The purchasing power of the dollar had so eroded because of inflation that, by the time he finished college in 1949, the same $25 a month that Ruth had found hard to live on in 1939 would buy 40 percent less. Being a victim of inflation makes one especially resentful of it.

When Bud Volcker took over at the Federal Reserve Board in 1979 to clean up a world financial mess, he had something else to draw upon from his Teaneck days. Paul Sr.'s tightness and frugality had earned him a nickname. "We called him 'High Pockets,' " said Richard Rodda , a friend who headed the township's recreation department. "I was the only one of two who called him that to his face. He thought it was very funny." "Old High Pockets," it turns out, was also a financial fireman of sorts.

Teaneck had decided to set up a city manager's office only because it found itself hopelessly, depressingly broke, living well beyond its means. The township had gone into debt building streets and other facilities before there were lots upon which to build houses. The problem was that the city had overestimated the economic benefits that would derive from the building of the George Washington Bridge. "Dad came in and did a complete reorganization financially," Ruth said. "He faced great opposition, too. A lot of people didn't want the city manager's form of government." Over several years with great effort, Paul Sr. worked the township through the financial crisis. Once his opponents tried to oust him after he made a nonpolitical appointment to a key job, but Paul Sr. remained firm and won a key test for the nonpartisan city manager's form of government in Teaneck. It was an important lesson for his son: stick with what you believe is right in the face of opposition.

Dick Rodda said Paul Sr. shunned the type of commercial development in Teaneck that other communities nearby had used in order to capitalize on completion of the George Washington Bridge. "He wanted the aesthetics," said Rodda. "He thought the bridge provided tremendous potential for creating an image for the community." While commercial development may have brought a broader tax base to pay off the debt. Paul Sr. preferred a tighter belt to tackiness.

Although his son was still young at the time, Bud Volcker learned about his father's crisis management later, as it became part of the town's lore. "The financial crisis of our city government was part of our youth," said Virginia. Paul Sr. held what many believe is a unique position; Teaneck has been credited with setting up the first nonpartisan city manager form of government in the nation.

Money itself never seemed to be central to the Volcker family, and the quest for too much of it was regarded as a little tacky. "Business always had a dirty name—if you had money . . . there was something questionable about it," Virginia told *Newsweek* magazine. Volcker himself said that those who spent all their lives trying to accumulate wealth may be missing its true essence.

It has always been ironic that the world's top money people, from New York to Bonn to Tokyo to Mexico City, would ultimately place their faith in a man who would hold their lifestyles and their money-making motivations in at least mild contempt. His main function in life turned out to be taking tough action that would curb their excesses in an effort to make sounder the pieces of paper they all exchanged and called *money*.

Actually, Volcker was not and is not antibusiness. More accurately, he looks with disdain on the greedier aspects of modern business practices and worries that some of these excesses are doing harm to the system. Excessive corporate salaries and bonuses, especially those taken by executives for firms that are losing money or market share or are laying off employees, grate on him as well.

In a speech at Harvard University in 1985, Volcker said that the "responsibility of government is to foster a climate of opportunity—an environment in which enterprise and ingenuity and personal initiative will flourish. We can't afford to lose those traditional American values of know-how and 'can do.' " But he went on to say that America could lose many of these values if "our acquisitive instincts" aren't kept within "accepted principles of law and policy." All this demands "a sense of personal responsibility and integrity rooted in a larger national purpose." In so many words, Volcker seemed to be saying that business leadership should be put to a higher test and that greed itself in business should be curbed.

NOT FAR FROM THE TREE

Tall as a reed and straight as an arrow, young Paul grew up in his father's footsteps in many ways. Years later, Volcker credited his father with instilling in him a sense of the importance of public service, as manifested by a sign on his father's desk: "You go into the public service for public good, not private gain." This ethic was to become part of Volcker's life more than even he might have expected. After he got a taste of it when he graduated from college, he kept returning to it willingly every time he was called, even though he could have made more money elsewhere.

His sisters in particular look back on those years in

Teaneck and see patterns of thought and threads of personality that prepared him for his public role.

"There was not a big stress on doing well in school, such as bringing home straight A report cards or anything like that," Virginia said. "There wasn't that kind of stress at all. It was more of an emphasis of doing good works, being honest. Government was very important, and you were supposed to work very hard to help people."

Also like his dad, Paul Jr. has a penchant for wanting to be by himself, either reading or thinking. Once, when he was four years old, he disappeared from sight. A diligent search led family members into the coal bin next to the coal furnace in the basement, where young Bud, then a towhead, had stolen off. It took them hours to clean him up, especially to get the coal dust out of his hair. Interestingly enough, it was one of the few times that his sisters remembered Bud's actually doing something that was frowned upon.

To see young Paul steal off to some hideaway to contemplate or read was not considered unusual, even when he grew older. Virginia remembers an evening in 1986 when she went to her brother's New York apartment for dinner. It was the first time that her grandchildren and his grandchildren had gotten together, and it was a festive occasion. "He made clam chowder, as my father used to do. They both liked to get in the kitchen and make up a big mess, and clam chowder was one of my father's things. After dinner, there was a lot of stuff going on with the kids. He got his cigar, and his daughter [Janice] was complaining because he was smoking while the kids were there. And he went into the other room and read his fly fishing magazine. Even though you know having the family around is important to him, he tends to disappear from it very frequently, which is sort of what my father did. I always remember my father behind the newspaper. I don't know why this was so. It could have been the old male pattern of withdrawing."

Barbara Volcker at times would find her husband

pulling off to the side, pondering for as long as 45 minutes without saying anything. There was nothing peculiar about this trait, she thought; it was his way of grabbing time for himself to think through problems dealing with the Federal Reserve.

"When I was home, he wasn't very talkative," said Ruth, who is eleven years older than Paul

Yet his parents thought he was plenty intelligent. They started him in kindergarten a year early, hoping that he could cope. Soon they were getting notes from the teacher saying that he wasn't participating in class. In a literal sense, it might be said that Paul Volcker flunked kindergarten. He actually began too young, and that was exacerbated by the fact that he was not an openly verbal child and, in fact, was more than a little shy. It didn't take long, however, for Bud to display his verbal skills in the Teaneck school system, although he has never completely gotten over his shyness. His marks always put him near or at the top of the class, despite the fact that he never had to study hard.

High school and college pal William Dippel said that, while his old friend was serious, aloof, and shy, he had softer edges than his father. "His father was a little tougher than Paul, not as phlegmatic. Outwardly, Paul was more relaxed."

To be sure, there was one way the son wasn't like the old man. When he took over the city manager's job, Paul Sr. was quoted as saying, "One of the things I don't like about city hall is that you see nothing but closed doors when you enter." Paul Jr., on the other hand, is a great believer in the closed door and the cold, secret stroke. He was one of the Fed's most secretive chairmen, feeling that this was one way to keep the market constantly guessing as to what the Fed was up to on a given day.

His father was so circumspect about public service that he refused to permit young Paul to remain on the payroll at 50¢ an hour in a part-time job in which he manned a street barrier and lantern and watched neighborhood kids sleigh-ride. Every time a snowstorm came, Rodda roped off "coasting streets" and hired high school seniors to set up the barriers and lanterns and keep watch. He picked Bud Volcker because he knew he was responsible and found he did one of the best jobs ever. But "High Pockets" Volcker called Rodda into the city manager's office and told him to fire his own son, saying others needed the job more and that he would need a new recreation director if Rodda refused. Rodda had to break the news to Bud, who took it well after being told orders came from his father. "I have the dubious distinction of being the only person who ever fired Paul Volcker from anything," said Rodda, who is now retired. All is forgiven. Volcker attended Rodda's retirement party in 1983.

THE MAKING OF THE MONEY MAN

Bud Volcker grew up at a serious time in the U.S. After the Depression came Would War II, the years when Paul attended Teaneck High School. Gasoline was rationed, and there were shortages of other materials needed in the war effort. There was none of the car-cruising of the 1950s, immortalized in *American Graffiti*, and students tended more to conservatism.

Paul was such a straight arrow that he rarely missed a day of school. His English teacher, William C. Moore, recalled that he was shocked by one incident in which, after being absent one day, Bud came in the next day with a note from his father. "Please excuse my son for being absent," it said. "I took him fishing. I figure a day spent fishing is worth a day at Teaneck High School." Since this was such a rare occasion, Moore dutifully excused young Paul.

It was also in high school that Paul held his first real job in finance as treasurer of Moore's Hi-Y Club, a group of boys who put on a show and handled the concessions at football games.

Teaneck was not exactly the center of the social

universe, in those days, despite its closeness to New York City. The Volckers didn't socialize with the country club set then, and Paul Sr. worked long hours. There were few places for entertainment; teenagers often gravitated to the Little Brown Jug, actually an old school where they could dance and listen to music. Paul himself was not a big socializer and, according to his family, had no girlfriends. "He was a late bloomer," sister Virginia said. She added that Bud's own shyness and penchant for staying by himself were emphasized by the fact that he had no brothers. "I think it made him more alone," she said.

As a boy, Paul Jr. did find a close friend in neighbor Harry Johannsen. Harry and Bud were virtually inseparable, playing with cars in the dirt or, later, baseball in the sandlot. Virginia observed that they didn't communicate much verbally as they played, yet they seemed to get along well. They were friends mostly in elementary school and drifted apart in high school. Fifty years later, Harry Johannsen expressed great admiration for his old playmate, calling him highly intelligent and honest. "He's done more for his country than any of those politicians," he said. "He's the most honest man in America."

Volcker concedes to being shy and, with a laugh, gives a reason. "My sisters used to beat up on me all the time," he said. While Volcker made this remark in an offhand manner, Virginia said it may be closer to the truth than indicated. His sisters did pick on him a bit, wondering why he didn't talk more.

Although Paul Jr. did have a tendency to withdraw in his younger days, he became more competitive within the family as he grew older. Family "arguments," more banter than real knock-down, drag-out disputes, became part of the scene on Longfellow Avenue. It was more like sport than anything else. Paul Sr. and his son would often be on one side and one or more of the daughters on the other.

The debates ranged far and wide, on everything from sports to politics, with young Bud finding an outlet to get over his reluctance to speak. "The one I still remember is that one argued for the army and the other for the navy,"

Virginia said. Virginia was a frequent participant in these discussions, but the late Louise was the most spirited of the lot.

Young Bud's technique in these family debates was to take the role of devil's advocate, asking enough questions and covering enough possibilities that he was sure that all avenues of a problem were covered. He learned later, of the central bank, that it is sometimes wise to play the role of the devil's advocate and test new policies before trying them on the public.

These intrafamily contests provided the first manifestation of the intellectual diligence with which the future Federal Reserve chairman would pursue public matters later in life. He is noted for digging deeply into questions, cross-examining staff members on the various implications of a particular problem or policy, and playing the role of devil's advocate if necessary to put it to a rigid intellectual test. Sportive argumentation turned into a useful technique in the hard world of monetary policy.

Athletic competition attracted Volcker as well. At six-foot-seven, he was a member of the basketball team and was, as Rodda described him, "a good high school basketball player. Bill Bradley he wasn't," referring to the former Princeton and New York Knicks star, now a U.S. senator from New Jersey. His height gave him an advantage over opponents, but he was not coordinated enough to make it to the big time.

He took a good-natured razzing for his height from some of his friends. One, Charles Gunner, blew terrible-sounding bugle every time Paul scored a basket. Although some called him shy, withdrawn, and nontalkative, Bud Volcker was a jock and "one of the boys" in high school. He never lost his love of sports.

The biggest sport of all, however, proved to be central banking. Bud Volcker left Teaneck imbued with some of the rudimentary values of this peculiar breed of national and international life. Those who knew him in the old days weren't surprised where he wound up.

5
TEAR UP YOUR CREDIT CARDS— PAUL IS IN THE SADDLE

After Volcker announced the Saturday Night Special, economist Alan Greenspan said that if the Fed were serious in controlling the money supply exclusively and abandoning all semblance of control over interest rates, it would be the most revolutionary change in monetary policy in the central bank's history.

"Volcker is a tough guy, although pressures on him to soften his position are likely to mount," Greenspan told *Time* magazine at the time.

Greenspan spoke with some knowledge of Federal Reserve Board history. As he would point out later, "the Federal Reserve is, despite its independence, a political institution. It is not unaware of the extent to which the Congress and/or the presidency is reacting to the board. What they endeavor to do is to swing policy within the range of certain parameters. They get neither extremely tight nor extremely easy."

Certainly historical evidence indicated that the Fed would sooner or later blink and ease up. Volcker, however, was determined not to repeat these past mistakes, even in an election year. He felt he had a commitment from the White House that he would be supported in his efforts to tame double-digit inflation. From the beginning, he knew that if his new policy was to be credible and effective, it would be a long, painful haul.

Then something happened to Volcker on the way to his goal. He unwittingly became involved in one of the Carter administration's politically motivated efforts to "take the pressure off interest rates," as one put it. Reluctantly, he let himself be talked into endorsing a mild form of credit controls, a terrible lapse of judgment.

It all happened because few people anticipated that the October 6, 1979, program would send interest rates soaring as high as they went in a few short months. Certainly Volcker did not. He was totally surprised. Certainly Carter did not. He was not only surprised but anxious, since he was running for reelection. The Iranian hostages and Senator Ted Kennedy (D., Massachusetts), his primary challenger, were already making his life miserable.

What made the Carter administration turn to credit controls was the increasing economic pinch of Volcker's tight money. Carter's economic advisors, who had tried everything short of wage-price controls, were casting about for a way to keep interest rates from rising in an election year.

Volcker made a terrible miscalculation. He saw Carter's interest in credit controls as a way to get some control over the federal budget deficit and make his own job of monetary policy easier. So he agreed to play ball with the White House if the mildest, least effective system of credit controls was imposed with his consent. If he had resisted this pressure, the job of bringing inflation under control in the early 1980s might have been a lot easier.

THE FED PLAN:
TIGHT MONEY CONTROL

Explaining this chain reaction and what it cost the country economically requires going back to October 6, 1979, and examining the dynamics of a highly technical Federal Reserve plan that, oddly enough, was designed to keep the independent central bank from being ensnared in the web of presidential politics.

No sooner had Volcker's program been announced than it changed the terms of the economic debate about the causes of and the cure for inflation. Now, suddenly, he had the entire world focused on the idea that it was entirely a monetary question and that controlling the money supply was the principal solution, just as Milton Friedman had preached. The odd thing was that the new policy was not the pure kind of monetarist economics Friedman has long espoused.

Into the center of this, Volcker put himself and the Federal Reserve Board as the agents for attacking the number one economic problem in the world. From this point on, every movement in the weekly money supply numbers would be put under a microscope by the financial markets and the press. It would be the Fed's job to get them under control as it had promised, or it would risk losing its credibility. Volcker loved it—not so much the attention as the intricacies and complexities of solving the problem. Although he talked constantly of the need for stability, nothing turned him on more than a crisis. It seemed to satisfy some deep, inner need to be put in charge of a crippled ship or a near-hopeless situation. As his wife Barbara said, "He feels greatly challenged by a crisis. I'd hate to say that it is something he enjoys, because no one enjoys a crisis. He becomes intellectually stimulated by a crisis. He doesn't go off half-cocked or anything like that. He's had a lot of experience with crisis management."

Henry Wallich, a fellow Fed governor, would not let the board forget that it was indeed a crisis. He spoke of parallels with the great German inflation of the 1920s, a debasing of the currency and the economy that many feel ultimately led to Hitler. "Henry talked about it a lot," said vice chairman Fred Schultz. "He said that as an eight-year-old boy in Germany in 1923 he understood what inflation was. Whenever he wanted to go to the community swimming pool, he had to pay a 150-billion-mark entrance fee. Henry had to go get a great big basket to carry the money to get into the pool."

The nation was ready for Volcker's attack on inflation. According to Charlie Schultze, inflation had become a bad experience for ordinary people; because prices were rising faster than wages, they could see themselves falling behind. As the Germans did before, Americans associated inflation with a reduction in their standard of living. This was a turnaround for a country that only a decade earlier didn't mind a little inflation and, in fact, saw it as somewhat necessary to a well-functioning economy.

Not everyone was prepared, for they had seen the results of previous tight-money episodes—idle capacity of factories, layoffs, human tragedy. Lane Kirkland, taking over for George Meany as president of the AFL-CIO, called it "the wrong move at the wrong time" and said it would not solve the inflationary problem. Further, he said it would violate a "national accord" that organized labor had reached with the Carter administration under which unions agreed to support the president's voluntary wage-price guidelines. The housing industry also complained and predicted that high interest rates would clobber home-building, as they usually do.

A DEPARTURE FROM PURE MONETARISM

Milton Friedman held back any compliments. In his *Newsweek* column, he wrote that "those of us who have

long favored such a change have repeatedly licked our
wounds when we mistakenly interpreted earlier Fed statements as pretending a change in operating procedure. I
hope that this time will be different, but remain skeptical
until performance matches announcement." Followers of
Friedman, such as Chicago economist Beryl Sprinkel, later
to become a top economic advisor to Ronald Reagan,
praised the new approach and said, if followed, it would
break the back of inflation.

Volcker didn't lose any sleep over Friedman's skepticism. Friedmanesque monetarism would put the money
creation process on virtual automatic pilot, removing the
Fed's ability to fine-tune it. A computer could in theory
handle the job. Friedman's theory held that there was a
direct mathematical link between the increase in the money
supply and economic growth. If the Federal Reserve would
supply funds to the economy on a steady, consistent,
gradual basis, economic stability sought by Volcker would
be achieved, and inflation would be tamed by denying it
the energy—too much money—to persist. With good
management of the money supply over several years, the
monetarists believed, inflation could be squeezed out of the
U.S. economy without a devastating recession. According
to the monetarists, the money supply doesn't just matter,
as most economists believe; it's the *only* thing that matters.

Friedman had good reason to be suspicious of
Volcker's alleged conversion to monetarism. It sounded
too good to be true, coming as it did from a man who had
demeaned the idea in the past, and Friedman was right.
Yet there was an undeniable shift in the Federal Reserve
system toward Friedman's theory at this moment. The Fed
never bought it hook, line, and sinker, but it had bit
enough to make its most monetaristic bank in the system,
the St. Louis Federal Reserve Bank, ecstatic over the
October 6, 1979, decision.

Volcker, on the surface, sounded sincere. "The classic
definition of inflation is too much money chasing too few
goods," he told the "MacNeil/Lehrer Report" on October

10, 1979. "And ultimately, as we bring the supply of money into accord with the needs of a noninflationary economy, you achieve a proportion between the amount of money and the amount of goods. And at that point, we can return to stable economic conditions, as far as inflation is concerned." This sounded enough like Friedman to make monetarists happy for a time.

But those inside the Fed, and Volcker himself, knew that a healthy dose of discretion would be required. Pure monetarism was too rigid. It did not take into account the many new forms of money being created in the economy. Nor did it make allowances for the imperfect operating procedures of the central bank or the need for flexibility when some mid-course correction was required. The Fed was not ready to put itself on automatic pilot as yet. For instance, it set a permissible range for interest rates (as defined by the so-called *federal funds rate*, the interest rate that banks charge each other for lending) to rise and fall. During the early months of the program, it kept moving this range upward as interest rates began to rise sharply, indicating that Volcker was serious about not controlling interest rates. When the Fed embarked on its program in 1979, it set the permissible federal funds range at 11.5 to 15.5 percent. By March of 1980, this had been increased to a range of 13 to 20 percent. Later, though, during a tumultuous 1980, the Fed fudged on its commitment to leave interest rates alone.

Robert P. Black, president of the Richmond Federal Reserve Bank and a member of the Federal Open Market Committee on October 6, 1979, said, "I don't think we ever got terribly close" to the rigid monetarism of Friedman. "A lot of people probably went along with Volcker's idea as a way to rationalize raising interest rates."

The policy was designed to be self-regulating in a sense. If the economy turned down, so would loan demand, and interest rates would fall; if business activity picked up, the demand for money would pick up, bidding up interest rates. In his first public appearance after the Saturday Night Special, Volcker gave the impression that he expected a slowdown to occur soon. He told the Senate Banking committee on October 15 that high interest rates could end almost as abruptly as they started. "If the economy slows down, and that becomes evident in the next few months, we could see this thing turn around quite quickly," he said. "It need not in that sense be a long period of time."

A CRISIS OF CONFIDENCE

Just the opposite happened. Interest rates continued to soar, with the prime interest rate charging past 15 percent at the beginning of 1980. At the end of February, it was 16.5 percent. This coincided with another crisis of confidence in Carter's ability to manage the economy. Carter's budget for fiscal 1981, which had been sent to congress early in the New Year, showed a deficit of $16.5 billion, seen by the markets as understated and unacceptable in a period of high inflation. Everyone—Carter, his economic aides, Volcker—was getting worried. In an extraordinary move, Carter yanked his budget and began working on a new one. A series of emergency meetings was held to work out a new anti-inflation program.

Carter's economic aides had been considering the idea of credit controls "to take the pressure off interest rates," as one put it. Excessive credit creation was considered to be a prime reason for continuing the inflationary momentum that held interest rates high.

Credit controls were a tricky proposition. The Credit Control Act of 1969 gave the president the power to "authorize" the Federal Reserve Board to implement the controls. Volcker, called into meetings with administration officials, made it clear the Fed was firmly against the controls. He also spoke for most of the other board members, who thought the controls would be terrible for the economy and difficult to administer.

Stuart Eizenstat, President Carter's chief domestic policy advisor, said Volcker drove a hard bargain. He refused to carry out the controls unless the president came up with a credible anti-inflation plan that included a balanced budget, Eizenstat said. "He held out for very substantial domestic cuts, which was very hard for a Democratic president," Eizenstat said. "That was the deal struck."

Volcker's recollection is different. He noted that the law under which credit controls were to be enacted was "peculiar," in that it technically appeared to give the Fed refusal rights to a presidential decision invoking the controls. As Volcker remembers Carter's attitude, "He and the administration were very gung-ho to make some gesture toward credit controls. He was also sitting still for a very tough Federal Reserve policy generally. He says, 'Look, it's going to help a lot politically to put on these controls.' The board said, 'We don't want to do that.' The administration said, 'It's terribly important.' We were willing to do something. We didn't want to do this Consumer thing. That's what he wanted to do. So we said that as part of the federal [anti-inflation] program, we will do as slow and ineffective a credit control program as we can think of."

Volcker did not recall the hard bargain Eizenstat spoke of, but noted that it was generally understood that any Fed agreement on credit controls was to be part of a package that included substantial reduction in the budget deficit, which Volcker found more important than credit controls.

Volcker puts this down as the biggest mistake that occurred during his tenure as a chairman, but he hedges on whether it was his mistake or the administration's, because of the way the credit control law, since repealed, provided dual responsibility.

Charles Schultze said the administration took Volcker into its planning on the anti-inflation program, and he participated more than Fed chairmen usually do in the formation of an administration's economic program. He said in his view Volcker did not breach the Fed's independent relationship with the executive branch. Indeed, there is ample precedent for such sessions between Fed chairmen and administration planners. "If you play the game, you've got to abide by the decision," Schultze said. "This was a time when everybody thought inflationary expectations were getting out of hand."

THE CREDIT CONTROLS FIASCO

Dutifully, on March 14, 1980, President Carter announced his new economic program—a budget in surplus, an oil import fee, and a system of credit controls to be announced at the Fed. The president said Volcker's tight-money program needed to be "reinforced so that effective constraint can be achieved in ways that spread the burden reasonably and fairly." Carter said that the central bank would establish controls for credit cards and other unsecured loans, but not secured loans on homes, automobiles, or other durable goods.

It might have been the way Carter worded his announcement that led to the fiasco that followed, but the Fed's credit controls were not quite as strong as had been indicated. The controls established the equivalent of a reserve requirement on consumer credit. Financial institutions would have to deposit with the Fed 15¢ for every new dollar of credit above the amount in existence on March 14. In addition, the program included voluntary measures to curb lending.

No one was prepared for the psychological effect the program would have. Credit virtually dried up. People began sending the Federal Reserve Board cut-up credit cards. It was one of the few times in modern American history that the people had truly responded to their leaders in Washington, even if it wasn't exactly the message the leaders wanted to deliver. The program also suffered from terrible timing. Consumer spending had already begun to suffer earlier in the year because of the pinch of higher oil prices and inflation on income. Consumer spending fell by 4.5 percent after inflation in the entire first half of 1980, and that softer spending had begun to show up before the credit controls were imposed.

The program "worked" so well that the economy collapsed. Real GNP (gross national product), output of the nation's goods and services discounted for inflation, dropped at a stunning 10 percent annual rate in the second quarter. This frightened almost everyone, especially the administration, when the collapse became apparent. But by the time the news came out, it was summer. The Fed dropped the credit controls swiftly and was happy for it, since financial institutions were grousing and the program was becoming difficult to administer.

The prime interest rate had hit 20 percent on April 3 and then started to decline in the face of what looked to be an extremely soft economy. By mid-August, it was down to 11 percent.

The credit controls created an odd yo-yo effect when combined with the Fed's monetarist policy. With the economy sinking like a rock in the second quarter, the central bank began pumping money into the banking system with abandon. A 10 percent drop in GNP was breathtaking and, if it continued at that level for several quarters in a row, it would undoubtedly mean a depression.

As an indication of how confusing the situation was, the Fed held a special FOMC meeting on March 7 and decided on a major tightening. Only eleven days later and four days after announcement of the Carter credit controls, it eased. It pumped more money into the economy on April 22, May 6, May 20, and July 9. Then it sat back and waited for the evidence. The money supply exploded in August, rising at an annual rate of nearly 20 percent. It continued upward strongly over the next several months. Volcker and the Fed turned 180 degrees, tightening in the fall of the year before the elections—and even more sharply afterwards. After a sharp plunge in the second quarter, GNP went up by 2.4 percent in the third quarter and by 3.8 percent in the fourth despite the Fed's tightening.

But the election was just around the corner, and to tighten to the degree called for by the Fed's own procedures set up on October 6, 1979, would have been highly controversial in an election year. According to one Federal Reserve source who did an analysis on the situation that year, the Fed did tighten before the election to try to bring the money supply under control, but it didn't get as tough as the targets called for. In other words, interest rates would have gone higher prior to the election if the central bank had been totally faithful to its operating procedure. Other Fed officials dispute this version.

The wild economic swings of 1980 led to a burst of money-supply growth that would last well into 1981 before it was brought under control. Considering that monetary policy acts with a lag, the credit controls of 1980 may have set the stage for the 1982 recession.

Two weeks before the election, the Fed squeezed tighter. Pad Caddell, one of Carter's top political aides, called Vice Chairman Fred Schultz, an old friend, and wanted to know "just what you guys were doing over there." Schultz responded that the Fed had no choice given the tremendous economic uncertainty in the markets, and Caddell let it drop.

Carter turned aside many of his political aides who were pressing him to speak to Volcker and ask him to make money easier at election time. They were also urging him to come out publicly and criticize the Federal Reserve. Carter did so only once, in a campaign appearance in Philadelphia, when he was asked about Volcker's policies. The president spoke of the rigidity of the Federal Reserve's monetary policy. This caused Volcker's backers in the money markets to rally behind him, and Carter found the criticism was not well received.

Volcker felt that, despite all the troubles with the economy during 1980, Carter was amazingly restrained. "Tight money went against Carter's populist instincts, but he largely left Volcker alone," said Eizenstat.

POLITICALLY RESILIENT

When Paul Volcker graduated from Teaneck High in 1945, the school yearbook said he "has an incredible knowledge of politics" and might one day become a town manager, too, just like his old man.

Volcker never thought of himself as a politician and, in fact, never ran for public office. But many who have watched him call him one of the best politicians in Washington. By this, they mean that he learned how to accomplish his objectives in an atmosphere of constant pressure and criticism, chiefly through good timing, moral suasion, and playing on the collective guilt of the political system for being wimpish in fighting inflation.

Milton Friedman has said that Volcker is nothing more than a loyal, capable, and completely flexible civil servant. "Any man who can serve successfully under Johnson, Nixon, Carter, and Reagan obviously has extraordinary qualities of political adaptability," he said in one of his patented putdowns.

Contrast that with the statement of Fred Bergsten, who was assistant secretary of the Treasury for international affairs in the Carter administration. Bergsten said the former president believes it was "the Ayatollah [Khomeini] and Volcker who cost him the election."

Like the hostages in Iran, Carter himself had become a hostage. With inflation screaming, he was not in much of a position to criticize his newly appointed Colossus of the Money Markets.

For all the vacillation and difficulties of 1980, Volcker emerged with his reputation intact. The money markets did not blame him for the credit controls, and they watched him tightening in the teeth of a presidential election.

Volcker knew that he had little choice. To maintain his credibility and the credibility of a program that was only a little over a year old when Reagan defeated Carter, he would have to tighten.

The amazing thing was that Volcker did not become a major political issue in 1980, considering the fact that his austerity monetary program had taken the nation through some rough times. Reagan, in fact, supported a strong monetary policy to battle inflation and would have nothing to do with any type of control program.

As 1980 came to a close, Volcker felt that he was about where he had started at the beginning of the year. Inflation was still skyrocketing, rising at 12.4 percent in 1980, and interest rates were still on the rise, headed back up to 20 percent.

He had played ball with the president, the man who had appointed him, and gotten burned. Now there was nothing left with which to fight inflation except his own tight-fisted monetary policy. Tall Paul seemed determined to stick with it as Ronald Reagan and his conservatives took over the White House.

6
THE EDUCATION OF A
CENTRAL BANKER

It was ironic that one of the most Keynesian administrations in U.S. history should pick as the head of the central bank a man who did not hold the philosophy in highest esteem. It wasn't that Paul Volcker was not steeped in Keynesian economics, such as the importance of the federal budget in influencing the economy and the need for national economic statistics to gauge the demand for goods and services. John Maynard Keynes, after all, had revolutionized economic theory and virtually invented the whole notion of macroeconomics. He had almost single-handedly written the language of modern economics. Volcker accepted many of the ideas of the famous British economist, but as with almost everything he encountered, he could not buy the almost romantic optimism that seemed to infect many of Keynes's followers.

Volcker made this distinction when asked if he was a Keynesian. "Whatever answer I give you, you will misinterpret or your readers will misinterpret," he said. "I'll give you a Nixonian answer: we're all Keynesians now—in terms of the way we look at things. National income statistics are a Keynesian view of the world, and the language of economists tends to be Keynesian. But if you mean by Keynesian that we've got to pump up the economy, that all these relationships are pretty clear and simple, that this gives us a tool for eternal prosperity if we do it right, that's all bullshit."

In fact, Volcker once told an interviewer that it was almost immoral for the government to accept a little inflation if it created jobs. Such a view would have been ridiculed in the halcyon days of the 1960s or even in the early 1970s when Richard Nixon was in the White House. It was Nixon, after all, who declared that "we are all Keynesians now." By the end of the decade, when inflation was raging and economic growth was stagnant, it became fashionable to question the way Keynesian economics had been interpreted and put into practice in the United States.

KEYNESIANISM VS. THE AUSTRIAN SCHOOL

Volcker's experience, his early days as a Federal Reserve Board staff member, and his service in the U.S. Treasury Department contributed enormously to his skepticism toward Keynesianism. But another major contributing factor was his education. As an impressionable undergraduate at Princeton University, he never encountered a professor who was a thoroughgoing Keynesian.

"I went through Princeton and took all their advanced undergraduate economic courses, and the word was never mentioned," he said. "That's a slight exaggeration, but not much of one. You learned nothing about the Keynesian method of analysis because the Princeton Economics Department was mainly out of the Austrian school. The guy who taught economic theory was out of the Austrian school; the guy who taught money and banking was out of the Austrian school. The others were not Keynesian. The course in business cycles didn't discuss Keynes, and in the course in economic theory Keynes wasn't even mentioned. Maybe saying Keynes wasn't mentioned is too strong. There was no body of analysis taught that was Keynesian."

The Austrian connection is important to the development of Volcker's economic theories. According to Harvard economist John Kenneth Galbraith, a good case can be made that the roaring inflation in Austria after World War I had more of an impact on economic thought than Germany's hyperinflation. It occurred under a young finance minister named Joseph A. Schumpeter, who went on to a brilliant academic career at Harvard. As Galbraith wrote: "The inflation was experienced or remembered by the men who were to compose the world's most distinguished coterie of conservative economists of the next generation—Friedrich von Hayek, Ludwig von Mises, Gottfried Haberler, Fritz Machlup, and Oskar Morganstern, all of whom also moved eventually to the United States. All shared with Schumpeter a profound mistrust of any action that seemed to risk inflation along with an even greater distaste for anything that seemed to suggest socialism. All were influential."

One of Volcker's economic teachers at Princeton—one he mentioned quite often to his friends—was Oskar Morganstern. "I know he respected his views," said Donald Maloney, a doctor who was Volcker's roommate at Princeton. Volcker pronounced his name with equal emphasis on both syllables—"OS-KAR." "I got a heavy dose," said Volcker. "He was very much of the Austrian school and he made some impression on me."

It was Schumpeter, a brilliant economist at Harvard, who told his students in the 1930s that depressions and recessions had beneficial effects. They were in the nature of a "good cold douche" for the economy, he said. Although Volcker may not have had this quote or Schumpeter precisely in mind, the idea was prominent in the Austrian

school. The recession that his tight money brought about in
1981–82 also had a huge cleansing effect and halted
inflation in its tracks.

When Volcker started at Princeton in the summer of
1945, the Keynesian revolution was well under way.
Keynesian economics had been employed by the administration of Franklin D. Roosevelt to increase federal spending to take up economic slack. World War II itself, which
resulted in heavy borrowing and spending, helped pull the
nation out of the Depression. Unlike in Germany, fear of
unemployment was much stronger than fear of inflation.
People feared idle resources and idle workers more than
they worried about the soundness of the dollar. Even as
Volcker began college and World War II came to an end,
the economics profession had a nagging fear that, with
wartime spending over, the economy might sink back into
depression again. But it did not, partly because of the
practice of Keynesian economics at the national level.

Lester Chandler, a retired economics professor at
Princeton, said Keynes's ideas were incorporated into the
courses of several professors at the time. In general,
though, it was not until the early 1950s that the Keynesian
doctrine spread like wildfire among college and university
economic departments across the country, becoming the
dominant economic philosophy.

Later, when Volcker did his graduate work at Harvard
University, he took a course under the foremost U.S.
interpreter and popularizer of Keynes, Alvin H. Hansen.
"It was Keynes pure and simple, but that was all right. He
was a very good teacher. The Keynesian things were
logical. . . ." But still vivid in Volcker's mind is a thesis he
read on Keynesian economics by a graduate student at the
Massachusetts Institute of Technology. "I remember the
message so well. Now that we've got Keynesian economics
and a little econometrics, that's it. We can manipulate
everything from now on, and the world will operate right.
And that was such a simplistic view of things." This,
according to Volcker, wasn't real Keynes. The British

economist never would have written such a simple little piece of work, he said, indicating that policymakers never made mistakes and banks always made good loans and with the right policies everything will always turn out right.

The author of that thesis was Lawrence Klein, later a Nobel prize-winning economist whose views matured with experience. One of Hansen's students was Paul A. Samuelson, who went on to write a famed economics textbook used widely in American college classrooms. Volcker was influenced by the New Economics at Harvard, and indeed he recognized Keynes's greatness. But he was never quite hooked in the way that others were.

One interesting speculation is that his Princeton experience had given him enough of a grounding in classical economics that he was not so easily swept away by this new activist theory of economics. Princeton also gave him something else, an emphasis on the more practical side of economics that stressed finding solutions. The purity of the theory was not as important as the solution to the problem.

POSTWAR PRINCETON: STILL ON THE STRAIGHT AND NARROW

Fresh out of Teaneck High School, Volcker did not have such weighty things as the Austrian School or Keynesianism on his mind. The war and the draft were more immediate concerns, as were financing his college education and establishing his own identity. It did not take young Bud long to establish his independence from his father, who wanted him to go to Rennselaer and major in engineering, too. But Paul Jr. applied to Princeton, where some of his friends were going, and was accepted. This move upset his father greatly and was a point of contention between the two for some time before Paul Sr. got over it.

High school graduates in 1945 weren't sure of what was ahead, so many decided to enroll in college so that, if they were drafted, they would have something to come back to later. When the U.S. dropped the atomic bomb to end World War II, Princeton students, in celebration, lit a huge bonfire on the common green. As for the draft, Volcker eluded it in his freshman year. He failed his physical because he was too tall.

The end of the war made a big difference at Princeton, as it did at other colleges. Donald Maloney, also from Teaneck, roomed with Volcker and noted that it made the entire student body more serious. Maloney said that the returning veterans had been around the world and had had many experiences to share with nonvets. "It had a big influence on us," he said. "They had a lot of different perceptions they shared with us about the world. We used to have a lot of bull sessions."

"Some of the veterans who played poker thought nothing of raising each other with an entire month's GI check," said Alvin Kracht, a Volcker friend. For Volcker, trying to get along on $25 a month, the gap in spending power must have seemed enormous, as it did to others from middle-class families. In those days, Princeton was relatively cheap, with tuition costing only a few hundred dollars a semester. Volcker settled in Dodd Hall, the cheapest dormitory on campus, with his friend Maloney and David McGrath, and practiced the kind of penny-pinching he had learned from his father.

"We rarely went to Nassau Street," where the action was, noted Maloney. "We were too young to drink at the Nassau Tavern. Our generation was very straight. I was in a dance band at Teaneck High. There was no drinking at the proms. Our band would play until 4:00 A.M., and we drank nothing but Coke."

Although Paul began to spread his wings a bit after leaving home, he still stuck close to the straight and narrow. "The ultimate straight arrow," said Kracht, now an advertising executive.

Volcker impressed everyone with his seeming ability to make high grades without much effort. "He would flip through the books and have total recall," Maloney said. "It must have been a photographic memory. He never gave the impression of having to work. We were straining and straining."

Yet he could be competitive. Maloney remembered that Paul considered himself in a race for the best grades with Dean Boorman, who attended the Woodrow Wilson School in his junior and senior years, as did Volcker. As Maloney remembers it, Volcker won out. "I think he was proud of beating out this fellow Boorman," Maloney said. If there was any such competition, though, it was news to Boorman. He said he didn't remember any such contest for grades with Volcker and said he knew him only casually.

For all his seriousness, Volcker also developed a fine, dry wit, and his friends thought him to be extremely funny. He did little dating in college, insofar as his friends can remember, and he developed a reputation for being shy.

Princeton in those days was an all-male institution, and, instead of fraternities, there were 18 "eating clubs," where students who joined could go to dine and socialize. Students were not pledged; they were "bickered." Volcker became a member of the Key and Seal Eating Club, not the most prestigious on campus in terms of the number of wealthy students who belonged. But it did have a few basketball players, including Volcker. These clubs were not as exclusive as fraternities. The university had a rule that students who weren't chosen would be parceled out.

Volcker was a sports nut, constantly talking about baseball or basketball. What he had in interest he lacked in talent. Because of his height, he was able to make the junior varsity and later the varsity team, but he never played much. "The standing joke was that he would wear out the top of his shoes sooner than the bottom because he had this habit of dragging his toe on the ground," Kracht said.

What Paul lacked in athletic ability he made up in academics. He made Phi Beta Kappa; he shone at the Woodrow Wilson School. According to the current dean,

Donald Stokes, the Woodrow Wilson School was inspired by the former president, who pushed the idea of "Princeton in the nation's service." Trustees in 1930 came up with the idea for a separate discipline that emphasized public service, with majors in economics, history, and languages. At the end of the decade, it had become a separate school.

The public service emphasis reinforced what Volcker had learned from his father. "You can't come near the place and not sense it," Dean Stokes said. Stokes said the school emphasized practical solutions of problems through a series of "policy conferences," in which students were locked in a room and given a complex, messy problem to solve. "Students have to do analytical work on the problem and pool their insights," he said.

LAYING THE FOUNDATION: EARLY MENTORS

One of Volcker's favorite teachers was Friedrich Lutz, a German-born professor whom Stokes described as "very clear-headed, inspirational, and very thoughtful. He was not a formal, technical economist. He was the kind of man who could give the sense of what economics could do." It was a tribute to Lutz that, years later, as head of the central bank, Volcker would credit him for turning him on to economics. Professor Lester Chandler described Lutz as pragmatic with a strong interest in international economics, qualities that Volcker himself possessed years later.

In a report written for the Twentieth Century Fund in 1947, Lutz and Norman B. Buchanan, an economist at the University of California, called for an expansion of trade in the postwar world, including relief and imports from the U.S. They called for curbs on inflation in trading countries, opposed nationalization, and favored realistic exchange rates for currencies. They said the major responsibility for world economic growth rested with the U.S. "Because of its importance as a market for other nations and as a source of investment capital, a stable American economy would be a major contribution to international stability."

This was not the hard-headed kind of hands-off economic policy that free-marketeers might have advised. It was activist, more in the Keynes mold, and it reflected the pragmatism of his teacher. Furthermore, it linked the fate of the domestic U.S. economy with the international economy, a theme that is almost a cliché now but was not so dominant in those days.

The teacher whom Volcker mentioned frequently to his friends, Oskar Morganstern, made his mark at the time when he wrote a book with the famed mathematician John von Neumann on the "game theory" of economics. It was an effort to use mathematics and the theory of games to develop a complex theory about economic behavior. All of economic life was interpreted as a kind of game in which the players made rational decisions to win or minimize losses. Morganstern had hoped to launch an entire new theory of economics that would develop a rational understanding of economic behavior based on mathematical game theory, rather than sweeping generalizations emanating from the mind of a Keynes. As he put it in a *Scientific American* article in 1950, "We all hope eventually to discover truly scientific theories that will tell us exactly how to stabilize employment, increase national income and distribute it adequately. But we must first obtain precision and mastery in a limited field, and then proceed to increasingly greater problems. There are no short cuts in economics."

Although Morganstern's ideas were interesting, they never gained the prominence he hoped (although game theory is enjoying a revival in economics). Still, his skepticism about the inadequacies of economic theories of the time and the measurement of economics doubtless had their impact on Volcker. Even today, Volcker freely expresses doubt when others make authoritative forecasts about the direction of the economy and presume to know the exact outcome of an action. Even more interesting is how this complex theory of establishing numerical relationships for people's behavior intrigued Volcker's intellect. It indicated an appreciation for abstract thought and organization and their application to human affairs. It was the type of thinking that would serve him well at the Federal Reserve.

As Volcker was completing his senior year at Princeton, he still did not know which career course he would follow. "I really had to scratch my head," he said. As it turned out, the decision centered on money. He wanted to go to graduate school at Harvard, so he applied for fellowships in law, business, and public administration. The Littauer School of Public Administration (now the Kennedy School) offered the best fellowship, $600 more than the others. He got acceptances from the law and business schools fairly quickly, but held out for several months before committing himself, as both schools pressed him to decide. Finally, in the nick of time, the Littauer School came through. "On that fellowship I could live," he said. "My great career decision was made. If it hadn't, I might well have been practicing law today."

ALL ROADS LEAD TO WASHINGTON

Volcker graduated with honors from Princeton in February 1949. He came to Washington looking for a part-time job, and the first place he walked into was the Federal Reserve Board's main office at 20th Street and Constitution Ave., N.W., where 30 years later he would be the boss. They told him there was nothing available.

"I just walked in and asked for a job," Volcker said. "They were very nice to me, but they said, thanks, but no thanks." It was February and Volcker wanted to work for six months until he went to Harvard.

He was not about to give up, though. He landed a summer job at the New York Federal Reserve Board as a research assistant in the research department. In his section, he was responsible for analyzing the supply and demand for money. He became so expert on one area that he wrote an article in the *Federal Reserve Bulletin.* "I was the world's leading expert on Federal Reserve float." Float refers to phantom money in the banking system; in the complex process of clearing out their reserve positions with the Fed, some checks are credited to a bank's reserve account before they are debited.

This demonstrated Volcker's technical capacity in the monetary field at an early age. He returned to the Fed for another summer of work after a year of graduate work at Harvard.

Then in 1951, Volcker found a job in Washington as a junior management assistant in the Treasury Department. "They had a project, but I remember nothing about why I got the job. They had hired some outsiders to look at econometric methods of estimating tax collections. It was my first introduction to econometrics. I was a statistical collector. Econometrics were pretty Greek to me, still are. You got a pretty good feel for how econometricians went about their jobs."

At Harvard, Volcker displayed the same seriousness he had at Princeton and impressed his friends with his ability to read and digest a book quickly, then dictate a paper off the top of his head. "We were a bunch of guys and a few women who were going for master's degrees and Ph.D.s," said Robert Kavesh. "There was this sense of camaraderie. Most of the people had been veterans of World War II. Volcker was not. He was a quiet guy. It was really not a boisterous group in that day. Most people were fairly serious. They had spent in some cases several years and in other cases a short time in the armed forces. . . . Volcker smoked cigarettes in those days. I remember that he smoked as much as two packs a day. In fact, I don't remember seeing him with a cigar in his mouth until several years later."

Volcker completed all requirements for a Ph.D. in economics at Harvard, except for his thesis. He had hoped to write his thesis at the London School of Economics because he had landed a Rotary scholarship to go overseas and study. Volcker completed all the course work but said the lure of London and Europe were too much for a young man. "He became bored with academic life," said a friend, attorney William Weber. He returned from London in the fall of 1952 ready to pursue a full-time career.

Volcker encountered a variety of economic doctrines in his educational career and gained an appreciation for flexibility. Modern economics as taught by Keynes appeared on the stage in 1936, and it was still very much in its infancy when Volcker went to school. So was the postwar system of fixed exchange rate for currencies, which Keynes helped negotiate at Bretton Woods, New Hampshire, in 1944. This system put the dollar at the center of the international monetary system and pegged the dollar's value in terms of an ounce of gold. In 1971, Volcker would play a role in ending this system.

No single doctrine dominated his mind. But, at heart, he was not a flaming liberal economist who was willing to prime the pump and tax and spend in order to cut unemployment to the bone, even if it risked a little more inflation. As his life developed, it turned out that he, like Keynes, would worry about the integrity of the currency.

As Keynes wrote: "Lenin is said to have declared that the best way to destroy the capitalist system was to debauch the currency. By a continuing process of inflation, governments can confiscate, secretly and unobserved, an important part of the wealth of their citizens. By this method they can confiscate arbitrarily. . . . Lenin was certainly right. There is no subtler, no surer means of overturning the existing basis of society than to debauch the currency. The process engages all the hidden forces of economic law on the side of destruction, and does it in a manner which not one man in a million is able to recognize."

In that sense, Paul Volcker is a Keynesian.

7
A TWO-BY-FOUR
FOR REAGANOMICS

The failure of the 1980 credit control experiment raised the intensity of Volcker's inflation-fighting campaign. The time for tinkering was past. Volcker knew that the Fed's credibility was at stake. By any objective standard of measurement, his crusade against rising prices had failed. A year after his famed money-tightening decision, prices were still rising more than 12 percent a year. If inflation wasn't brought under control, he reasoned, the public would soon reach the conclusion that the central bank had lost its nerve. The possible consequences were grim: either Latin-style inflation or another depression or perhaps both in succession.

Troubling questions haunted him. How long would it take for this tight-money policy to do the job, and could it be done without a recession? How far would interest rates have to go? Would the financial system crack under the strain? Would he do severe long-term damage to the economy by raising borrowing costs so high that businesses would not invest? Was the instability in the money supply in the first full year of the new technique an indication that it was inherently flawed? And, perhaps more fundamentally, how much and for how long would the political system, and ultimately the American people, tolerate tight money before they put so much pressure on the institution that he had to relent?

The answers to most of those questions were elusive because Volcker knew that he was sailing uncharted economic waters. He and his colleagues at the Fed, though, were convinced that the upcoming bout with inflation, which would increase unemployment and bankruptcies, would be extremely painful for the economy. Although they did not plan or encourage a recession, they would not be surprised if the economy sank into one. "No one was under any illusions," said Volcker.

Up to this point, the nation's political leaders had been fairly tolerant of this anti-inflation program because they had no other choice. According to the polls, inflation was the number one concern of Americans, and the White House and Congress found it difficult to dump on the only general left on the field of battle. Any bitterness Jimmy Carter may have felt over what Volcker did during the 1980 campaign was silenced by Carter's perceptions that his own anti-inflation program had failed and only Volcker's had a chance of working.

The sense of national economic crisis gripping the country silenced most critics of the Fed. From both a political and an economic standpoint, the time was ripe for tough action. The late 1980 tightening was excruciating. On September 25, the Fed raised its discount rate .5 percent to 11 percent, and then, right after the presidential election, it boosted this key lending rate again by a full percentage point, to 12 percent. By year's end, it had pushed the discount rate to 13 percent. Large banks that borrow frequently from the Fed were forced to pay a 3 percent surcharge. More important, market interest rates began skyrocketing as the Fed withdrew reserves from the banking system through its open-market operations. On December 21, 1980, the prime interest rate hit a record 21.5 percent. Homebuilders began sending Volcker two-by-four wooden blocks to protest tight money's effect on their industry. They poured into this office in the thousands, all with a message: ease up before our industry dies.

After Carter lost the election and became a lame duck, Volcker saw his opportunity to crack down on inflation without bringing the wrath of the White House down on hs head. Economically—and politically—it was time to move. Fed chairmen have a way of going underground before an election and reemerging with full vigor just afterward.

But Walter Mondale did not at all appreciate what happened.

Although that 21.5 percent interest rate came after the 1980 election, the incoming president, Ronald Reagan, saw it as future political fodder. He would use it again in a presidential campaign, when he ran against Walter Mondale in 1984. Mondale said that the central bank overdid tight money after the election. "They really jammed on the brakes," he said. "They sent those interest rates up to 21.5 percent. As Reagan kept reminding them, that became cancer to me in the latter campaign [1984] because they could compare 21.5 percent on January 1981 with whatever it was after that, and that's what people remembered." Volcker felt the freedom to tighten after the election, Mondale said, "but it was a price I had to pay because it became Carter's mark."

A few of Volcker's Fed colleagues began to worry that the new onslaught might cause the economy to crack. Nancy Teeters, a Carter appointee to the Federal Reserve Board, began dissenting from moves to boost interest rates after the November election, worrying that her colleagues were risking another depression, a worry that was not uncommon in the economics field. For several months, she filed lonely dissents, questioning whether the Fed's monetary targets were too tight and whether the relationship between the growth in money and the growth in the economy had broken down. As it turned out, her objections were premature.

WOULD REAGAN BACK VOLCKER?

A point of anxiety for Volcker was whether the new Reagan administration would support him. The Fed chairman had a few friends inside the new administration dating back to the Nixon years, but most of the key players were newcomers who preached either the doctrine of supply-side economics, calling for a sharp cut in tax rates to recharge the economy's creative energies, or monetarism, calling for a slow and steady increase in the money supply to keep inflation in check. Reagan's new economic program would marry these two ideological strains, even though many economists, with great prescience, had warned of their inherent incompatibility.

From the beginning, the Reaganites eyed Volcker with suspicion. In the middle of the 1980 race, Edwin Meese, a campaign stalwart who would later become a White House counselor and still later attorney general, implied that Volcker should resign his post. Economists whom Reagan listened to in the campaign, such as monetarists Milton Friedman and Alan Meltzer, were sharply critical of Volcker's record, arguing that wide swings in the money supply were making things worse.

But the key was to be Reagan's attitude. In a pinch, would he back Volcker? Individual members of an administration can criticize the chairman of the Federal Reserve Board and still not precipitate a crisis, but if a president chooses to join in the Fed-bashing in an active way, it's a different story. Although the Fed is technically independent, outright presidential opposition could probably force a change in the central bank leadership, a change in policy, or perhaps a change in its independent status.

The whole anti-inflation program would come crashing down if the new president chose, at any point over the next few years, to oppose the central bank openly and aggressively. This Volcker knew. Considering the attitude of some of Reagan's advisors, it was more than just a cause of idle concern.

Reagan's victory provided a new challenge for Volcker. In addition to the problem of a runaway money supply and accompanying rising interest rates, he had to contend with a fiscal policy that many economists said was written in bright red ink. The new president came into office fostering a revolutionary fiscal policy calling for a 30 percent reduction in federal income taxes and new tax breaks for businesses to spur lagging investment in the U.S. The program embodied supply-side economics, which held that individual tax rates had risen so high in the U.S. that they had retarded work effort, investment, and job creation. Furthermore, some of the supply-side theorists who took high positions in the U.S. Treasury Department believed that the program would be relatively painless from a budgetary standpoint. If enacted, they said, the program would generate an economic boom. As national income increased, this would bring in enough tax revenue to ensure that the budget deficit would not become a massive problem.

Volcker recognized instantly that the new program had the potential for causing big budget deficits and making his job of controlling inflation more difficult. On the other hand, he knew that a nonelected Fed chairman should not try to subvert the will of the American people. In voting Reagan into office, the people had implicitly endorsed these tax reductions.

The Fed chose to walk the proverbial tightrope. Volcker went to Capital Hill and said the tax reductions had merit as long as they were accompanied by compensating spending cuts. In theory, this was administration policy, too, but it did not work out that way. In a comment that rankled the combative new Treasury secretary, Donald T. Regan, Volcker said tax cuts should be made contingent on spending cuts. If the tax cuts were not balanced by spending cuts, the chairman said, the Federal Reserve would have no other choice but to keep monetary policy tight.

Volcker was ready to reach out to the new administration, but he was not about to cave in to it. Some of Reagan's economic advisors moved quickly to set up an early meeting with Volcker. Martin Anderson, a Californian who served admirably in Reagan's campaign, decided to be the go-between from his post as chief of the president's domestic policy staff. First on the agenda was to be a meeting between the new president and Volcker. Where to meet became a problem of some delicacy and diplomacy.

"We offered to have the president go to the Federal Reserve," Anderson said. "We thought that would be nice. Right? Wrong. Volcker was so upset about that, didn't like that idea at all. The reason was that it would in some way be seen as compromising their independence if the president went over there. On the other hand, there seemed to be some reluctance on his part to come to the White House. So finally we came up with a Solomonlike solution—to go to the Treasury."

So, three days after his inauguration, Reagan and a retinue of White House economic and political aides strolled out onto Pennsylvania Avenue for the short walk next door to the Treasury Department, attracting a parade of tourists behind them. It was a rare thing for Reagan, indeed any president, to do because of the security problems, but in the weeks before he was shot, the new president was not nearly so cautious.

It was little more than a get-acquainted session, but in retrospect it probably was a better meeting for Volcker than it was for Reagan. There, over lunch in Treasury Secretary Regan's executive dining room, they traded anecdotes and talked about fishing. Reagan told Volcker that he hoped that he would move to reduce the price of gold, a comment that his economic aides wished he had skipped. The new president, Volcker quickly learned, was very much a "gold bug" who believed that the gold standard was key to international economic stability and that the price of gold itself had an important monetary function. Did Reagan know that across the table from him was one of the men responsible for ending the gold standard back in Richard Nixon's administration?

Had not Murray Weidenbaum, chairman of Reagan's Council of Economic Advisors, interrupted, Volcker and Reagan would have continued in this vein. It was time to discuss monetary policy, he said. But that, too, became a high general discussion, with Reagan's aides stressing a Federal Reserve policy that would continue to bring down inflation with economic growth. Weidenbaum also brought up the issue of Federal Reserve independence. "I raised it on behalf of the administration and urged the president to accept it," Weidenbaum said. "It was the first meeting ever between the president and Volcker. I thought it would be useful to have a statement endorsing its independence." Reagan agreed to permit Weidenbaum to make a public statement to that effect, although the president had in the past expressed some doubt about the Fed's independence. Privately, he would continue to express his doubts about it in the future.

The first meeting set the tone of future—and infrequent—sessions between Reagan and Volcker, but later they were held in the White House, and some were even held in Reagan's private quarters in the East Wing. Weidenbaum said the early meetings never accomplished much because so many people were in the room, so that later Reagan and Volcker sometimes met alone. The president called him by his first name and obviously liked and admired the Fed chief. To the extent these meetings were not confrontational and resulted in no pressure being put on the Fed chief, Volcker emerged as the victor.

GRADUALISM AND
THE "ROSY SCENARIO"

Inflation in 1980 soared by 12.4 percent, a slight improvement over the 13.3 percent of 1979, and in the early months of 1981 it appeared to be continuing in the 12 percent range. The prospect of Latin-American–style inflation began to worry many economists, including many at the Federal Reserve, and the incoming administration saw the U.S. economy on the brink of collapse. Newly appointed Budget Director David Stockman had just penned a memorandum with Representative Jack Kemp (R., New York) warning that the U.S. faced an "economic Dunkirk" if it could not get its tax and spending house in order. The president echoed that feeling when he made a speech from the Oval Office on February 5, 1981. He said the U.S. faced "the worst economic mess since the Great Depression" and called for $13 billion in immediate spending cuts and another $50 billion in fiscal 1982. "We are threatened with an economic calamity of tremendous proportions, and the old business-as-usual treatment can't save us," Reagan said. "We can leave our children with an unrepayable massive debt and a shattered economy, or we can leave them liberty in a land of opportunity where every individual has the opportunity to be whatever God intended us to be."

When the president announced his new program on February 18, complete with details of where he would like to see budget cuts made, he left the control of inflation up to the Federal Reserve. But what he outlined was clearly a gradualist policy. If the Fed followed its monetary targets, the administration said, inflation would fall softly from 11.1 percent in 1981 to 8.3 percent in 1982, 7 percent in 1983, 6 percent in 1984, 5.4 percent in 1985, and 4.9 percent in 1986. It was a pure Friedmanesque kind of forecast. With a gentle fall in inflation, it said, the economy would avoid a recession and rise solidly, by more than 4 percent, for five years in a row. In view of the economy's troubles, this projection was promptly labeled the "rosy scenario" by many economists and members of Congress.

"The administration supports the announced objective of the Federal Reserve to continue to seek gradual reduction in the growth of money and credit aggregates during the years ahead," the administration's proposal said. "Looking back, it seems clear that if a policy of this kind had been successfully followed in the past, inflation today would be substantially lower and would not appear to be so intractable. . . . With the Federal Reserve gradually but persistently reducing the growth of money, inflation should decline at least as fast as anticipated. Moreover, if monetary growth rates are maintained, then inflationary expectations will decline. And since interest rate movements are largely a mirror of price expectations, reduction in one will produce reduction in the other."

One administration official said gradualism was "the only real shot we had of correcting inflation without a real recession." Sprinkel clung to the hope of gradualism, and so did the top supply-sider economists in the Treasury, Norman Ture and Paul Craig Roberts. Looking at the situation from his monetarist background, however, Sprinkel feared that the central bank would be tempted to push too hard and then stay with its tightness for too long, driving the economy into a recession.

Gradualism was an official Fed policy, but only sort of. Each year, the central bank set its targets for growth in the money supply. These targets were expressed in terms of percentages. The only problem was that that permitted a great deal of leeway. For example, in 1981, the Fed's target for growth in the basic money supply, the amount of currency in circulation plus demand deposits, was 3 to 5.5 percent. Anything within this range was permissible, so it gave the central bank discretion in where it wanted to land—or, at least, so it seemed. Its ostensible plan was to reduce the upper and lower limits of this range over a period of several years so that inflation would be gradually "squeezed" out of the system. Yet one could hardly call gradualism a policy that permitted the Fed to let money grow by 5.5 percent one year and perhaps 3 percent or even lower the next.

Even at that, Weidenbaum and Volcker worked out a loose plan that called for a 50 percent reduction in growth of money over a five-year period. As Reagan's chief economic advisor noted, it was an extremely general commitment, so that the Fed could in theory achieve these reductions at any time. Weidenbaum said that Sprinkel submitted a proposal that would have committed the Fed to year-by-year reductions in money growth, but that was acceptable neither to Weidenbaum nor to Volcker.

Gradualism died in 1981, but the jury is still out on whether Volcker conducted an act of premeditated murder or its demise was accidental. The recession that began to develop in 1981 was the direct result of an historic economic policy mismatch. Reagan's tax cuts pushed on the accelerator as Volcker's tight money pushed on the brakes. The brakes won, hands down, and the uncertainty caused by these powerful opposing forces added a few percentage points to interest rates, too.

Volcker did not place great faith in gradualism. It looked good on paper, perhaps, and at first blush it seemed to be a sensible course to follow. But to him, it offered a painless cure for inflation that did not seem plausible, and from a semantic standpoint it made the Fed's anti-inflation policy sound wimpish to money markets expecting strength and resolve. "*Gradualism* is a very comforting word meaning that nothing very drastic is going to happen," Volcker said. He felt a 5- to 10-year plan to cut the rate of inflation in small, imperceptible amounts was unworkable and probably not credible. He had seen economic surprises and attitude changes destroy such carefully designed plans in the past. Gradualism to him was akin to the kind of economic fine-tuning that had brought monetarist critics down on him earlier.

THE PRAGMATISTS
VS. THE IDEOLOGUES
OR THE FED VS. TREASURY

To Volcker, inflation in 1981 had reached crisis proportions, and to whip it called for strong, immediate, and clear action. Don't tap it gently. Whack it. Crisis management would demand no less.

In view of Volcker's reputation as a pragmatist who favored strong reactive moves to current economic problems, it was no surprise that he ran afoul of the more ideological economic thinkers that came to Washington with the new administration. Monetarist Sprinkel and supply-side economists Norman Ture and Paul Craig Roberts encouraged their new boss, Treasury Secretary Regan, to criticize the Federal Reserve for failing to keep the money supply growing at an even keel. Ture kept warning Regan that the volatility in the growth of the money supply was keeping interest rates higher and could cancel out the effect of Reagan's tax cuts. Sprinkel echoed that complaint and feared that the Fed would stay with its tight money for too long as the year progressed, eliminating the gradualist approach.

Regan's Treasury was the hotbed of criticism against the Federal Reserve. At the White House, Weidenbaum, Anderson, Stockman, and chief of staff James A. Baker III took a more moderate stance. Anderson believed that open warfare against the central bank was counterproductive. Not only would it cause the Fed to stiffen its resolve, but it also would frighten money markets that were already skittish over the Reagan tax-cut program.

"There were times we were quite irate with the Fed," Ture recalled. "We didn't know what those guys were up to. We wondered why they couldn't be team players or why they didn't seem to understand the Reagan program. When the words got to be hot, that raised some concern in the White House. Volcker was called over, and there would be handshaking with the president. Then it would be quiet for a while. At times, there were explicit orders from the White House not to be so overtly critical of the Fed because it might upset the markets."

The Treasury secretary met with Volcker once a week and often talked to him by telephone, but real communication between the two barely existed. Regan felt that Volcker was talking right past him and not being totally candid. Volcker found Regan erratic; he could say one thing at their private meetings with each other and then go out and make a public statement that was just the opposite.

The lack of trust stemmed from the fact that both were, and are, strong personalities. Regan came into office as a former Wall Street executive accustomed to having his own way, and Volcker, a strong-minded leader in his own right, was known as the second most powerful man in Washington. Regan, a multimillionaire, once told a reporter that he had enough "fuck-you" money to relieve any anxiety about losing his job, giving him room for aggressive pursuit of his aims as secretary of the Treasury in the new Reagan administration. He would ask about Volcker, "Whose horse did he ride in here on?" To Regan, that meant Jimmy Carter. Once he disparagingly referred to Volcker as a "lap-dog" who would do Regan's bidding.

If only it were true. Volcker was standing in his way. As one former Reagan administration official who knows both men closely said, "I don't think Don Regan could have tolerated being the second most important spokesman on anything."

Volcker, on the other hand, had been the big boy on the economic block in Washington since Jimmy Carter put him into office. Now, suddenly, this inexperienced stockbroker with definite ideas of his own about monetary policy was challenging the sanctity of his domain, accusing him of following "erratic" policies that kept interest rates higher than they should be. It was enough to make Volcker wary and to stiffen his back. It also caused him to make other alliances within the new administration, notably with the bright new budget director, Stockman, and with his old friend, Weidenbaum.

In his first week on the job in January 1981, Regan made the rounds of the senior staff at Treasury, meeting with a few of them at a time. At one of these sessions, he blurted out, "I don't know why we need an independent Federal Reserve Board." The remark took a few in the room aback, but it revealed a Regan attitude that later was to become a sore point with Volcker when the Treasury chief launched an internal study into ways to restructure the Fed.

The first few months of the Reagan administration solidified the rivalry between Regan and Volcker. Both men needled each other in public constantly. A few days after Regan spoke of erratic monetary policy in his confirmation hearings in Congress, Volcker went up to Capitol Hill and blamed these fluctuations on inflationary expectations and the lack of help the central bank was getting from the budget policy. Volcker found Regan good at criticizing him for last month's monetary policy. But when Volcker asked Regan what he would do next, the treasury chief had no recommendation.

The great irony is that, when the FOMC decided in May to clamp down even tighter and withdraw bank reserves from the economy to curb inflation, Regan told Volcker that the Federal Reserve was making the right move and, in fact, should have moved sooner to counter a rising money supply. This support surprised Volcker, who himself had wondered at the time whether the Fed was being too tight. The May 1981 clampdown was one of the roughest the Fed had taken during the entire three-year experiment with trying to control monetary aggregates. He expected Regan to complain vociferously because the economy was weakening and Reagan's tax-cut program, which was headed toward passage in Congress, would not take effect until October 1.

EXIT INFLATION, ENTER RECESSION: AN ACCIDENT?

The May 1981 tightening was the beginning of the end for the inflationary bubble that had been lingering in the United States for the past several years. It set in motion the forces that would soon lead to the worst recession since the 1930s. Through most of the rest of the year, the central bank would keep the pressure on issuing reserves to the banking system.

The May decision came after the money supply jumped at an annual rate of 14 percent in April and the broader measures of the money supply—M2 and M3, which included certificates of deposits and other time deposits—were growing well beyond the Fed's targets. Even though the economy was slowing down, the Fed said it looked strong enough to pose a risk of "excessive expansion in money and credit as the year developed." Significantly, it said that it worried about a big rise in the velocity of money (the rate at which a newly created dollar is used, or turned over, borrowed and spent, and spent and borrowed to create new economic activity). The rate at which the Fed supplied dollars to the economy could be adjusted up and down depending on how much economic activity the newly created dollars caused. Still, once the money is pumped into the economy and causes more spending than expected, it requires time for the Fed to adjust. Central banks have always lived in mortal fear of causing a situation in which the money they add to the economy is turned over rapidly, driving up inflation in the process. As it turned out, the fear of an excessive expansion in the money supply and a sharp increase in the turnover of money was unfounded.

Even to this day, some who played a role in the ultimate conquering of inflation believe it was accidental. Lyle Gramley, who for five years was one of the seven board governors, said that in hindsight that appears to be the case. At the time, the central bank did not take into account adequately the fact that in an era of high interest rates the same amount of newly created dollars would spark fewer transactions. Gramley believes that the nation-wide introduction of interest-bearing NOW accounts in 1981 so distorted the money-supply figures that it caused the Fed to be tighter than it would otherwise have been. Essentially bank demand deposits that earn interest, NOW accounts became a problem because they were counted as part of the basic money supply known as M1. The Fed used M1 targets as a guide for its policy actions because it represented money that could be converted quickly into cash and used in transactions. Money held in savings accounts would not be put to use in buying and selling immediately, so it was given secondary importance in determining what the Fed would do from day to day and month to month. The Fed was more interested in money that people were apt to spend immediately; too much of that could be inflationary in an already inflationary climate.

NOW accounts created an enormous measuring head-ache for the central bank. First, it changed its definition of the money supply to include NOW accounts, calling it M1B. Since part of this money was savings and part was money that would be spent right away, the central bank conducted studies to try to sort out how much fell into each category so that it could make sensible policy deci-sions. Gramley said that, in retrospect, it underestimated how much of it was pure savings and overestimated how much would be used for transactions. As a result, the Fed took a good look in May 1981 and saw that the money supply was surging again; the 14 percent rise in the April figures confirmed that. So it began withdrawing reserves from the banking system, launching a new wave of tight money.

Although it was clear that Volcker had probably adopted a policy that was actually tighter than he desired, it is not so apparent that this extra tightness was what brought on the recession. To maintain market trust in him,

Volcker had only one option and that was to tighten; the money markets were judging him daily on precisely how he responded to rises in the money supply. Credibility in this climate was essential, even if it was bought at the price of being excessive. Volcker pooh-poohed speculation that the Fed's policy in early 1981 was too tight because of miscalculation. If the Fed was holding the money supply a percent or two tighter than it intended, "that was all within the range of uncertainty anyway," he said. The chairman never bought the idea of an accidental recession.

Steve Axilrod, the Fed's chief staff director at the time, disagreed that the inflation-taming recession was an accident. "The bald fact is that this recession was inherent in getting rid of inflation," he said. If the Fed had not acted, he said, more severe inflation would have occurred because "you wouldn't have calmed inflationary expectations enough."

The Fed's tighter new policy did not bring sustained administration support. With the president's new tax cut clearing Congress and the economy weakening, the Fed-bashing began, coming chiefly from the Treasury Department. Economist Paul Craig Roberts said Volcker and company had deliberately set out on a panicky course because of excessive fear of Reagan's economic program. The same fears were echoed in Wall Street financial houses, where analysts saw the Reagan program as a deficit machine that could bring back massive inflation if the Fed kept money too loose.

Volcker was deeply concerned about the budget deficit and did not mind telling anyone who would listen. The Reagan administration accused him of harping on the deficit to deflect attention away from his monetary policy, but that did not deter him.

ROUND TWO: VOLCKER VS. REGAN

The Volcker-Regan feud intensified as a result. "They would always grumble about each other independently," said William Niskanen, who was a member of the President's Council of Economic Advisers. "One thing that Regan did not like was that Volcker would testify in Congress and feel free to criticize administration policies of all kinds, particularly the budget, and he would be seen as a statesman. But if Regan criticized monetary policy, he would be jumped on. Regan clearly chafed at that. He felt Volcker wasn't following the rules. Volcker would just grumble about the Treasury's ad hoc explanations about what was causing interest rates to be so high, such as blaming the Fed for a volatile money supply."

Stockman's chief economist, Larry Kudlow, thought the Treasury criticism was too harsh, as well as wrong, and suggested to his boss that he and Volcker get together to discuss monetary policy. Through Stockman, who began to see eye to eye with Volcker on monetary policy, the Fed chief would have an outlet for getting his point of view expressed with more sympathy in meetings of top administration officials. Stockman shared Volcker's view that the budget deficit was potentially a disaster for the U.S. economy and would make monetary policy difficult if not brought under control. Later, his celebrated book on the Reagan budget would detail just how out of control the federal budget had gotten under the new president.

Schultz and Kudlow also set up a regular meeting among second-level officials at the Fed, Treasury, and White House, mainly in an effort to get some dialogue going and relieve some of the tension. Often it deteriorated into a Fed-bashing session, with supply-side economist Roberts of Treasury engaging in most of the sharp criticism.

In complaining that the Fed's monetary policy was too volatile, Regan once said that the Fed wound up in "too many sand traps." Trying a little levity to ease the tension between the two men, Volcker had his staff draw up an elaborate chart of a golf course. Each "golfer" was a country. Volcker had each country with a more volatile money supply than the United States' wind up in a sand trap. As it turned out, the U.S. had the best record, so it wound up in the hole. Regan responded by sending the Fed chief a box of cigars.

It would be unfair to suggest that passage of the president's tax-cut program in 1981, along with inadequate budget reductions, had no effect on Volcker and bore no relation to the tougher policies he pursued. Quite the contrary, the budget deficit was on his mind all the time. He knew that the government would have to borrow the shortfall from the private markets, eating up savings that might be used more productively and bidding up the cost of money. He knew that this would put pressure on the central bank to buy more government securities in the open market, therefore monetizing the debt and adding to inflationary pressures. He could not foresee at the time the degree to which foreign capital would begin pouring into the United States to offset the government deficit. If he had, he would have been more concerned about the impact of the big deficits.

But Volcker also was reacting to technical matters involving money growth, maintaining his agency's credibility both within the U.S. and worldwide, and trying to curtail current inflation. Efforts to paint him as the devil who gleefully killed supply-side economics came mostly from the supply-side economists, hardly an objective group. Volcker's immediate aim was not to counter a budgetary or tax-cut problem, nor was it to make the Fed's policy mechanistically pure from an economic standpoint. Rather, he was out to eliminate the massive expectations of inflation that had persisted in the United States for most of the 1970s and the early 1980s.

Gramley said that during the critical period of monetary slowdown, from the middle of 1980 to the fall of 1981, he continued to make the same speech. The Fed, he said, would persist until it knocked inflation in the head, despite the pain that it would cause. After this speech, Gramley asked each audience for its forecast for inflation for the next five years. "Their answer would be 10 to 12 percent, or something like that," he said. "I told them, 'you people haven't heard anything I've said tonight. It was a waste of my time to come here. You don't believe me, do you?' They would say, 'No, we don't. We've heard these strong words from the Federal Reserve before, and we know that when the chips are down you guys will cave. This has happened for years and years and years.' It wasn't until the fall of 1981 that I saw the signs of the beginnings of a major breakthrough."

The Federal Reserve's 1980 tightening was cold-turkey monetary policy, and Volcker was its architect. When the year was over, the Fed reported that the money supply had expanded by only 2.25 percent in 1981, a full percentage point below the lower end of its own established range and the smallest annual increase in money growth since the early 1960s. It had gained the market's respect, all right, and it finally began to change people's expectations about rising prices.

As the economy began to sink into a recession in the final quarter of 1981, the Reagan administration stepped up its criticism. On October 6, Regan went public and called its policy too tight. He called on Volcker to make more money available to lower interest rates so that businesses "could take advantage of the tax cuts and start rebuilding." A day later, he said, "We're at a crossroads now. We don't want them to jump on the gas and pump money into the system," but added that tight money "could exacerbate the situation."

Volcker, addressing an American Bankers Association convention, said the economy was "moving sideways" and added that "inflating the money supply now would only aggravate the situation." But the economy was doing more than moving sideways. It was beginning to drop. As the economy began to stall, inflation began to fall. The United States wound up 1981 with an inflation rate of 8.9 percent, the lowest since 1977. And the best was yet to come.

But the country was also left with an odd, contradictory, and self-destructive economic policy. The administration had succeeded in cutting taxes, boosting the defense budget, and making only partial progress in curbing the momentum of federal spending. The nation had an extremely loose fiscal policy and an extremely tight money policy. One of the results of this was that bond rates reached extraordinarily high levels in relation to the rate of inflation. Triple-A bonds yielded between 12.5 percent and 15.49 percent in 1981. The nation's businesses were forced to engage in more short-term borrowing to finance their expansions. The clash between fiscal and monetary policy also kept other interest rates high, and eventually it contributed to an extremely strong dollar as foreign capital was attracted by the high rates of interest.

Volcker was an accessory to a mismatch of national economic policy that would in future years lead to an erosion of the American standard of living. Barry Bosworth, an economist at the Brookings Institution and former Carter administration official, said Volcker missed an opportunity to speak forthrightly to Congress and the American public about the dangers of the Reagan program. He never put his prestige on the line in a way that would have forced Congress to reassess the entire program, simply because the highly respected chairman of the Fed did not think it was a good idea.

Steven Roach, an economist at Morgan Stanley and a former Fed staff member, said that Volcker's comments about the Reagan program were standard Federal Reserve complaints along these lines: monetary policy can't do the job alone, and fiscal policy therefore must play a role. "I can't remember a Fed chairman who hadn't said that," Roach said. In his mind and in Bosworth's mind, the chairman should have been more direct and more dramatic in giving the American people, Congress, and the whole international community one straightforward message: Look, this will not work considering what I am trying to do. If you want inflation to remain under control, maintain our standard of living, and have a more stable economy, you will scale back this program. We at the Fed cannot live with it in its present form.

Volcker defends himself against such charges by pointing out that he said from the beginning that tax cuts should be accompanied by compensating spending cuts, so that the deficit would not get out of line. Further, he told Congress that the spending cuts should come before tax cuts. In addition, Volcker as a nonelected official did not want to put the Fed in the middle of a political confrontation with the White House. The new president was popular, and his program was popular, and it would be pointless to oppose it, Volcker reasoned. In fact, he found meritorious some aspects of the Reagan tax-cut program.

Volcker was distressed when, in an effort to get the tax-cut bill approved, the White House engaged in a "bidding war" with various factions of Congress seeking various concessions. He thought that the White House passed up a chance to obtain a sensible compromise when it rejected a plan by Representative Dan Rostenkowski, Chicago Democrat and chairman of the House Ways and Means Committee, to make the second and third year of Reagan's tax cut contingent on a reduction in inflation. That would have avoided converting the bill into the huge Christmas tree that it became.

Volcker and his vice chairman, Fred Schultz, went to Congress during the debate on the tax bill to warn members of potential consequences of approving such a bill without enough spending reductions, but by this time it was too late.

Although the nation would be left with an unbalanced economic policy, at least Volcker had made substantial progress in turning the corner on inflation.

FED INDEPENDENCE: STILL INTACT

Years after the fact, Volcker felt the president was a lot more tolerant of his tight-money policies than other administrations might have been. Unlike Jimmy Carter, Reagan had not proposed some economic gimmick like credit controls designed to take the heat off the White House, nor had he confronted Volcker directly in public. Volcker also did not take all the credit for breaking the back of inflation in 1981. He credited Reagan for his refusal to back down during the air controllers' strike. Reagan chose to fire striking controllers rather than pay their demands—a big psychological move. It definitely helped hold down wages. That had as much to do with breaking inflationary expectations as his tight money, the Fed chief said. "The significance was that someone finally took on an aggressive, well-organized union and said no," Volcker said. "I think that did have a psychological effect on the strength of the union bargaining position on other issues—whatever the issues were."

Volcker may have gotten off easy because of the president's detached management style. The president found it difficult to confront someone he felt had ill served him, and he was not conversant with the technicalities of sophisticated monetary policy. Because his advisors were divided on how to deal with Volcker, the Fed chairman found himself with plenty of room to operate.

One of Volcker's axioms about Fed independence is simple: never let an administration in power get you in the position where it expects you to do what it wants to do.

He had been burned on credit controls, and he wasn't about to let himself be drawn into another political agenda. He did not want to follow the examples of past chairmen who, he felt, let themselves step across the line. Around the Fed was the memory that former chairman William Miller had permitted administration officials to apply direct pressure on the central bank, with former Treasury chief W. Michael Blumenthal telling Fed officials to be tighter. Fed officials recalled that, during the Nixon administration, White House aides put in a call to the director of research, Charles Partee (later a board member), and told him that at the end of each day he should ask himself what the Fed was doing to keep the money supply at an acceptable rate.

Volcker also did not want to engage in the process of dispensing policy advice to the administration, fearing that once he began to be identified as a consultant he would become a captive of the policy and be expected to deliver the type of monetary policy the administration wanted, regardless of whether that policy was in the national interest. Some Fed chairmen of the past liked to play this game—Arthur F. Burns, Jr., for one. Burns denies that he ever yielded to political pressure, even though some of his critics say that he opened the monetary floodgates in 1972 to help Nixon's reelection.

For Fed chairmen, distance from the White House was good. The wisdom of the 1979 policy was beginning to pay off: it insulated the central bank from the political process more than even Volcker would have dreamed.

8
THE FED CONNECTION

It helps to have connections. They don't guarantee success, but for the talented and the aggressive they
bring valuable experience at an early age, daily contact
with important people, and a faster career climb.

In 1952, Paul Volcker had connections. They weren't
impressive connections, but they were good enough for a
young man who had the mental equipment to parlay them
into something bigger. His father knew a banker in
Teaneck who was willing to put in a good word for young
Paul to a vice president he knew at the Federal Reserve
Bank of New York. The vice president in turn gave
Volcker's name to the manager of the research department.

TRAINING CAMP: THE NEW YORK FED

Thus it was that young Volcker got his job interview with
Robert V. (Bob) Roosa, manager of research for the New
York Fed. Paul had just returned from his year of study at
the London School of Economics. He was weary of

academics and eager to begin his career in the financial world at the New York Fed.

"It was not the usual route for screening people," said Roosa of the way in which Volcker landed an interview. The fact that he had not finished his Ph.D. during his studies at the London School of Economics was a strike against him, but not a big one. To his credit, Volcker had two summers of solid work at the bank behind him and his own knowledge and intelligence and a good academic record. As Roosa recalled, "When we got to talking about his interest in the United Kingdom and its economy, I found he was well up on it and knew as much about it as I had been reading in our reports. I told him, 'Why not come to work in our British desk?' " Although Volcker hadn't finished his dissertation, he had become thoroughly familiar with the British economy in his classroom studies and in his observance of daily economic life in London. He once told a *Time* magazine reporter, "My lasting memory of the place is the repeated need to put shillings into a heater in a small, cold flat at night."

Although the Fed official didn't know it at the time, Robert Vincent Roosa, a pleasant, garrulous economist who had won two Bronze Stars for his work as an intelligence officer on General Omar N. Bradley's staff during World War II, would become Paul Volcker's mentor. Without this connection, as became apparent later, Volcker's life would have taken an entirely different turn. Roosa admired this young man for his intelligence and humility, as well as for his ability to learn quickly. Years later, he would find himself referring to Volcker as "my boy."

Similarities between the two men also added to their mutual respect. Both had brilliant academic careers and were members of Phi Beta Kappa, but, unlike Volcker, Roosa had his doctor's degree, which he earned from the University of Michigan in 1942. Roosa had started as an economist in the New York Fed in 1941, but schooling and the war forced him to leave that post until he was able to resume it in 1946. He was an expert on Federal Reserve operations and a stickler for technical details. Although he was a Keynesian economist, he had strong respect for the freedom of the markets. Later in the 1950s, as he became an important spokesman for the central bank, a commentator said that he "argued eloquently against forced-draft efforts to spur the country's economic growth, particularly through attempts to restrain interest rates artificially."

While monetary policy is made at the Federal Reserve Board's headquarters in Washington, the New York Fed was, and is, the center of the financial world. Here is where the Fed carries out its key job of buying and selling government securities in the open market, the chief process by which it adds reserves to the banking system and, in consequence, affects the nation's money supply. Here is where it buys and sells foreign currencies to raise or lower the value of the dollar. The center of the world's largest capital market and the nation's biggest money-center bank was an ideal place for a young economist to cut his teeth.

Working in the Fed, though, gives one a different outlook from, say, working in a brokerage firm or at a commercial bank. As Volcker would learn, it is the nature of the work. "The focus is on what the monetary and banking system does to affect the stability of the economy," Roosa said. "Growing out of that is a deep concern over the risk of inflation and how it can distort relative values. It becomes an institutional mentality, and once you have lived with it you tend to absorb it." It is the same with central bankers everywhere, Roosa said. He recalled the story of a Swedish Labor Party official who was put on the central bank there; within a year, "he was raising the discount rate, making speeches on how much the government was spending, and taking steps to curb the money supply." Even the most liberal can become conservative working for the Fed.

Steven Roach, an economist at Morgan Stanley who also worked at the Fed, said his central-bank experience "gave me a strong discipline in understanding how the economy works and how the Fed works. It forced me to understand the need to be more eclectic. Blind acceptance of any particular economic ideology doesn't really carry any sway in policy circles." One learns that markets have their own momentum, often react whimsically, and rarely respect policymakers in Washington, he said.

Those who work for a long time at the Fed soon pick up its institutional biases, including the notion that it must remain as independent as possible while still learning to work with the political system. Roosa had a little saying he used all the time: "The Federal Reserve must be independent with, but not independent of, the government." Some thirty years after Roosa had hired him and after he had been through the Washington wars battling for Fed independence, Volcker's former boss held a dinner in his honor. When Volcker got up to speak, he referred to this old Roosa principle. "I grew up as a member of the Roosa school, and I'm proud of it," he said.

For the next five years, Volcker labored at the New York Fed under Roosa's tutelage. Working with him at one time or another were some of the nation's most prominent economists, including Henry Kaufman and Albert Wojnilower, both of whom went on to high-paying positions on Wall Street.

At about the same time, connections also played a big role in Volcker's personal life. Don Maloney, his old college roommate from Princeton and fellow Teaneck native, had been dating a bright, witty, attractive graduate of Brown University named Barbara Bahnson, daughter of a general practitioner. Maloney constantly talked about his old friend who was away studying in London. When he found that Volcker had returned, Don and Barbara went out to the Volcker house to welcome him back. Barbara Bahnson is only five-foot-seven, and when she saw the Volcker family, all of them over six feet tall except for Mrs. Volcker, she was a bit taken aback. "Everybody was standing up around the table, and Paul was toasting the queen. He was the tallest man I ever met and certainly the funniest," she said. From that point, she decided to go after him. She had some friends put together a cocktail party and invited Paul.

"It was an uphill fight for two years," she said. Barbara offered to do some typing for him. Not long after, they began going out together. "It was really clinched when I started going out with someone else," she said. That brought the relationship to an important crossroads. Even at that, he wasn't the one to pop the question. "I did," Barbara said. "I really went after him." She felt that Volcker may have been reluctant because he thought that, as an economist, he would never make a lot of money to support a family. They were married on September 11, 1954.

"Those were the days when economists were really in the back room wearing green eyeshades," she said. "He started out at the Fed making about $3,000 a year, and I was working at Colgate-Palmolive Company at about $2,500. The difference for the amount of education was not that wide."

Once Paul told her that he would never amount to much and would probably wind up working in some dark office as an economist, wearing his green eyeshade and making only $6,000 a year. This statement did not reflect humility or a lack of ambition so much as an accurate assessment of the general state of employment of economists at the time. Barbara Volcker said that many young economists who went to work for banks found that they had to supplement their salaries by teaching. But as Paul and Barbara were to learn, this situation was to change dramatically over the next several years.

The postwar expansion of the American economy, along with the development of macroeconomics itself under the influence of followers of John Maynard Keynes, made economics one of the hot new professions. "I date the age of the economist from 1955 on," said Volcker friend Robert Kavesh. "After the Depression of the 1930s and World War II, a lot of people were very pessimistic about the economy. There was a postwar boom, then a recession in 1948–49. A lot of people said the system was going to collapse. It didn't. There was the Korean War and a second recession in 1953–54, and people said again the system was going to unwind. It didn't. Almost from the beginning of the recovery, a burden was lifted from the economy. Companies began to hire economists, not only to look at current economic and financial conditions but also to plan for a more optimistic future. In New York, big bank mergers began. They hired vast numbers of economists. People paid attention. The whole Federal Reserve system expanded the number of economists and also gave them titles."

The New York Fed, located in the center of Wall Street, suited Volcker's talents perfectly. "I used on him the same kind of medicine I used on everyone else," Roosa said. "Everyone wanted to get into the foreign field, but I told him you really can't fully understand markets until you learn the U.S. market, so come on down to the end of the hall and work on domestic markets." So Volcker moved from the British desk and into domestic research under George Garvey and began writing a monthly article on money and security for the Fed's publication.

In 1953, when Roosa was asked to take charge of the Fed's all-important trading desk, where it actually buys and sells securities, he realized that he was going to have to make regular written reports on open-market operations. "I realized it would be a wonderful opportunity for Paul," he said, so he pulled him into the Fed's key open market operations. In addition to writing these reports for Roosa, Volcker was put on the so-called "order desk," where he gave orders for government securities to the primary dealers with which the Fed deals on a daily basis. In this Volcker participated in something called the "go-around." When the central bank decided it wanted to buy securities from its official list of dealers (such as commercial banks and government securities firms), Volcker would place a call for orders and would receive quotations from dealers. The Fed would get the orders.

"It was great training," Roosa said. "It's where you really learn about markets. I met with the dealers every morning before the market opened, and often Paul would be with me. The interesting thing is that you could reach a conclusion about what might happen in the market next week. But you realized that the market is bigger than anybody. Nobody can be so sure of himself that he can give a clear projection on what's happening and all the forces involved."

Throughout this period, Volcker was able to observe firsthand the jealousy and occasional conflicts that occurred between the New York Fed, which was there on the firing line, and the board of governors back in Washington. Partly because of the suspicions back in Washington that the New York Fed was overstepping its bounds in monetary policy, Roosa instituted the written reports. Also, there were daily phone calls between the two, with the Treasury listening in.

VALUABLE EXPOSURE
AT CHASE MANHATTAN

Roosa went back to research in 1956. Volcker, by now an expert on Fed operations and public and private finance, had caught the eye of some powerful financiers. In 1957, David Rockefeller lured him to Chase Manhattan Bank and made him a financial economist. There were no green eyeshades, and his salary was in the range of $12,000 a year, twice what he had told his wife a few years earlier was the most he would ever make. (In 1987 dollars, this was the equivalent of more than $40,000.)

Volcker was happy in his work and his personal life. His daughter Janice, was born in 1955 and James in 1958. Jimmy's birth was difficult, and learning that he had cerebral palsy posed another challenge for Paul and Barbara, who by now had settled into a comfortable home in Plainfield, New Jersey.

At Chase, Volcker worked in the economics department for John D. Wilson, who said Volcker proved to be an excellent worker who expressed himself well in writing. Also working at the bank was old college pal Kavesh, who said that Volcker "did a bang-up job" for Chase and that "almost from the beginning, the bank was amazed at the ability of this man, and they used him tremendously. Even while he was a junior officer, he asked to dine with the senior officers so as to be available for lunchtime conversations about the Treasury financings, Federal Reserve policy, and the like. In those times, knowledge about financial economics was very, very primitive. You had a few bank letters. You had almost no discussion on radio or television about financial or economic matters. Volcker, who had this unique ability to simplify and present things, was really a very valuable person for the bank to have. They really used him because he was the one at the bank who knew Federal Reserve stuff."

One of Volcker's key jobs was as Rockefeller's right-hand man on a congressionally established but privately funded Commission on Money and Credit, which studied and made recommendations on the nation's financial structure. With some high-powered financiers as members, the commission took two years to complete its report, thus giving Volcker valuable exposure in the financial world. One person who sat on the commission recalled that Rockefeller needed Volcker's expertise. "Paul would be sitting beside him and rescuing him," he said. "I remember once when Rockefeller made some absurd statement. I was sitting next to Paul and passed him a note that said, 'Let's see how he digs himself out of this one.' Paul wrote back, 'What are you trying to do, get me in trouble?' " From all indications, though, Volcker was a loyal staff man to Rockefeller.

Kavesh said that Volcker especially liked George Champion, then the senior executive officer of Chase

Manhattan. "He was an old-fashioned banker," Kavesh said. "He didn't believe in making loans to foreign governments. His idea of banking was that banks take in deposits and then make good loans. That's really the old kind of banking. He was an arch-Republican and unalterably opposed to Keynesianism and all that. But Paul liked him and respected this kind of raw integrity. And he liked Paul, even though he knew that Paul's political persuasion was different."

Later in life, Volcker would jokingly say that if he were in charge of making loans for a commercial bank, he probably would be like Champion and not make many.

THE TREASURY IN A DEMOCRATIC ADMINISTRATION

Though Volcker in subsequent years would be known as apolitical, it was not always that way. "I was brought up in a Republican family and considered myself a Republican," he said. "I kind of got frustrated with the Republican Party in the 1950s. Adlai Stevenson came along, and he was very attractive to people of my generation. I decided I was for Stevenson." It was Stevenson's cerebral approach that attracted her husband, said Barbara. In the 1960 race between John F. Kennedy and Richard Nixon, Volcker served as treasurer of a Kennedy committee in Plainfield. According to Barbara, he received contributions from only six people, which wasn't bad, considering there were only 11 registered Democrats in the precinct. "I remember going to vote, and the people at the polls would say 'Here comes number nine,' " Barbara Volcker said.

In 1962, his old mentor Roosa entered his life again. Roosa had left the Fed and gone to Washington to become undersecretary for monetary affairs in the Treasury Department. He called Volcker to ask him to join him as part of the Kennedy administration in a new research division, and Volcker went on the payroll as director of the Treasury's Office of Financial Analysis, in charge of long-range financial planning. Roosa recalls that Volcker's official affiliation became a point of contention, as it was thought that he was a Republican. Roosa said that the only way they could get Volcker's name past the political appointees was to point out that Volcker had served on a "Republicans for Kennedy" committee in 1960—which was inaccurate. All along, Volcker had been a registered Democrat.

Despite these early troubles, Volcker soon became an important figure in the Treasury Department. The secretary of the Treasury, C. Douglas Dillon, instantly recognized his talents and made him his chief speech writer. "He became a star with Dillon as soon as he got a whiff of his ability," said J. Dewey Daane, who was Roosa's chief assistant.

As he headed for Dallas in November 1963 to face an assassin's bullet, President Kennedy named Daane as a member of the Federal Reserve Board and Volcker as Roosa's $20,000-a-year assistant. Kennedy's assassination forced Volcker into his first real experience with government crisis management. The Treasury moved quickly to close the stock exchanges and the banks in New York to guard against financial panic. They made calls to all the banks (they had trouble reaching Rockefeller). "Paul certainly got a little example of how to deal with a fast-breaking situation," Roosa said.

In the 1960s, western Europe had resumed its role as a major economic power, and Japan was in the process of becoming a major industrial power and challenger. The demand for dollars around the world was still exceptionally strong, and when President Kennedy came to power, the U.S. began to worry about a serious dollar drain that threatened the nation's gold supplies. In those days, governments could exchange dollars for gold, which was worth $35 an ounce. This fixed value was at the heart of the postwar monetary system established at Bretton, Woods, New Hampshire, in 1944.

The Kennedy administration took a number of key steps in the 1960s to relieve the growing pressure on the international economic system. The top ten industrial countries set up the Group of 10, essentially the finance ministers of participating nations. This group not only approved a plan in which the countries that got into balance-of-payments difficulty could borrow from each other, but began to coordinate economic policy as well. For the next two decades, this body would be active in a string of international monetary crises and plans to counter them. Another coordinating group set up about the same time was the so-called "Working Part 3" of the Organization of Economic Cooperation and Development based in Paris. Roosa had arranged for swaps of currencies among the industrial powers to stabilize currency values and even pioneered a nonmarketable U.S. Treasury bond that only other governments could buy. These securities were known as "Roosa bonds." Despite their short-term benefit to monetary stability, in the longer run the U.S. was criticized for releasing so many dollars into the world economy.

As one of the Treasury's top officials, Volcker was pulled into the various crises, frequently traveling overseas. When Roosa came up with the idea in mid-1963 to plug the dollar drain by imposing an interest equalization tax, he assigned Volcker the task of working out the details. He wanted to slap a 1 percent surcharge on all interest and dividend payments made to the U.S. by foreign nongovernment borrowers. This would "make the effective interest rates here 1 percent higher without having recourse to a Draconian monetary restraint that might have pushed the economy into recession," Roosa said.

"Intellectually, it was kind of interesting," Volcker said. "It was part of my introduction to the realities of the political process. You had all these nice concepts, and you were aiming to make it work just as generally, as impersonally, as the market itself, and then you ran into the fact that reality was a little tough and compromises had to be made. For instance, some guy had a chain of hotels and wanted to get some more investment in them, and he had two senators on his side. It may not look so nice according to the theory, but they were going to be exempted, you know. It wasn't as bad as some of the things I've seen since, but it was an introduction to that process."

Volcker prepared the proposal and the reporting forms, even though his heart wasn't in the idea from the start. When it was announced to a storm of opposition from abroad, he was dispatched to Europe to try to calm things down. As with many such proposals, they achieved the short-run goal but did not solve the long-run dollar problem. It was only the beginning of a series of restraints on capital outflows. The tax, later repealed, and these other restraints helped create the Eurodollar market, in which trading in dollars occurred outside the reach of U.S. regulators, Roosa said. This huge market added to the international currency instability of the time and hastened the day when it would break down, in 1971. Roosa said that a New York banker told him at the time that "we'll make a fortune on this. We'll do all our dealings in dollars in Europe."

With the international monetary system not functioning well, top Treasury officials began thinking of ways it might work better. Volcker participated in these discussions, which resulted in the launching of a study by the Group of 10, in cooperation with the International Monetary Fund. But it would be years later before this study bore fruit. It resulted in the creation of a new reserve currency unit, the special drawing right or DSR, known as *paper gold*, which governments would use to settle accounts with each other through the IMF.

Volcker supervised the Treasury's offices of financial analysis, debt analysis, and domestic gold and silver operations while working under Roosa. For his work he received the Arthur S. Flemming Award as one of the ten most outstanding young men in the federal government.

But when Roosa left the Treasury in late 1965 to make some money at Brown Brothers Harriman, an investment banking firm, Volcker did not get the top job as undersecretary of monetary affairs; instead, it went to Frederick Deming. His wife remembers feeling disappointed that he did not get the post.

ROCKEFELLER AND CHASE REDUX

In late 1965, Volcker resigned the Treasury job and accepted a job with his old employer, David Rockefeller, this time as vice president for "forward planning." Since Chase was a huge multinational bank facing questions of where, when, and how much to expand around the world, Volcker became involved in the international side of the bank. But working at Chase this time around was different. The bank was embroiled in internal political struggles, and Volcker obviously was not seen as part of the future senior management. "He wasn't too happy," said friend Kavesh. "At that time they were living in Montclair, New Jersey. The warning signal that went up was that he started to spend a lot of time gardening and started coming home at reasonable hours. Paul is happiest when he is working. I don't think Chase knew what to do with him at the time. It was just a bad slot. He was dealing with a lot of people who were management types and of a behavioral science orientation. They were speaking a kind of jargon. This was not for him. He wanted to get on with things."

Volcker felt stuck in his job at Chase, but did not get the impression that Rockefeller feared or distrusted him. Volcker was regarded chiefly as a high-powered staff person. "David Rockefeller had a tendency to park people from time to time," Kavesh said. "There were a few people whom no one knew what they were quite there for. They seemed to have some unique talent. It was almost as if there were some inventory of talented people that might be used at one time or another."

For Volcker, being back at Chase was not the same as dealing with the major economic questions of the day, making key decisions, and meeting with foreign finance ministers and central bankers in faraway places. Those things would come again, though. Bob Roosa would make sure of it.

9
A KNOCKOUT PUNCH
FOR INFLATION

Marble is the perfect facade for the Federal Reserve Board's Washington headquarters. It feels cold, strong, and distant. If one finds tourists trying to get into the building, it is because they are either lost, in search of a rest room, or very unusual sightseers. The Federal Reserve Board does not encourage casual visitors.

There is a palpable sense of insularity here. Walking into the building from the C Street Entrance, you encounter a huge area open to the second floor. It is somewhat like an atrium, except immediately in front of you are huge stairs that lead straight to the second floor and directly into the huge boardroom where the governors meet. Each step, however soft, echoes off the interior marble. The boardroom itself is long and airy, with golden fleur-de-lis wallpaper. In the center is a 25-foot-long oblong table, one of the largest in a city known for large tables. At the end of the table, to the right, the chairman sits. Behind his chair are plaques commemorating the fact that the combined chiefs of the Allies met here during the Roosevelt-Trident conference of May 1943 and set the pattern for cooperation through the remainder of World War II.

The outside world seems far away in this hushed chamber. The lives of real people are told on matter-of-fact economic charts hanging in the room like icons. Hardship in debates and analysis usually is expressed in abstract numbers; that is the only way the board has to get some relative sense of what effects its actions are having. Anecdotal evidence does not count for much here.

"GENTLEMEN, GO TO YOUR CORNERS"

In 1982, the serenity of this place was shattered by the cacophony of farmers, car dealers, homebuilders, small businessmen, small-town bankers, and others, all seeking a letup in the high interest rates that were pushing them toward, if not into, bankruptcy. Car dealers sent keys in coffins, and protesting farmers formed a ring around the building. Members of Congress squealed and introduced resolutions against the Fed. Some proposed impeachment of Volcker and his board, while others simply sought to remove the Fed's power to control the money supply or to restructure the central bank. These severe measures never got anywhere.

By January, Paul Volcker's clampdown had done its job. The economy had already sunk into a deep recession in the fourth quarter of 1981, with real GNP declining at an annual rate of 4.9 percent. As 1982 arrived, real GNP was still dropping at roughly the same pace, and unemployment and bankruptcies rose along with the political temperature. But Volcker had not wrung inflation out of the system to the degree that he wanted. Consumer prices in 1981 climbed by a hefty 8.9 percent, although they were below double-digit levels for the first time since 1978. Although the economy in many respects groaned under this monetary onslaught, in his mind it was not the time to let up.

The heat was on Volcker. According to Budget Director David Stockman, Senate Republican leader Howard Baker (later to become Reagan's chief of staff) said at a leadership meeting at the White House that "we're going to have to put our foot on Volcker's neck." House Democratic Leader James Wright of Texas called for Volcker's resignation. Almost every Volcker appearance on Capitaol Hill in that fateful year resulted in criticism from senators and representatives seeking a lowering of interest rates.

Old Washington hands had reason to believe that such pressure would work. The record of previous administrations indicated a close correlation between the Fed's monetary policy and the type of monetary policy sought by the White House. Stick it to them in public, it was believed, and the central bank would respond as it had in the past.

In response to this, the tough Paul Volcker, the one who fights back when backed into a corner, burst into the open. It started when President Reagan said at a press conference in mid-January that an upsurge in the money supply was sending "the wrong signal" to money markets and might be delaying the effect of his tax-cut program. "I know a great many industries have the plans already for modernization and expansion," the president said. "I think there's a little caution at work, and perhaps part of that is waiting to see what the Federal Reserve Board is doing." When asked about calls for Volcker's resignation, Reagan gave a neutral answer, unlike in the past when he had supported Volcker publicly. On January 20, Treasury Secretary Regan followed up and criticized the "uneven pattern" of money supply growth and said the Fed needed to sharpen its controls.

Volcker made a speech a week later and declared there would be no backing down. He blamed high deficits, not just monetary policy, for high interest rates. "The Federal Reserve has no way of offsetting the financial market pressure associated with excessive deficits," he said. "Pushing more money into the system simply to finance the Treasury would only serve to heighten fears about inflation and the future course of interest rates." Take that, Ronald Reagan and Don Regan.

Not only that, but Volcker continued to harp on the deficits in his testimony before Congress and said he frankly wished the president would show more concern. As for Regan, Volcker said he doubted whether the Treasury chief's prediction that the economy would come "roaring back" in 1982 would come true. Volcker threw the administration only one crumb, and it proved to be little more than that as the year progressed. In announcing the Fed's monetary targets for the year ahead—2.5 to 5 percent for M1—he said the central bank would aim for money growth at the top part of the range, which was what Regan was seeking. Secretly, though, Volcker's Fed had voted to permit absolutely no growth in M1 in the first quarter, a decision that would contribute to the continuation of the recession.

This was monetary policy at its most macho, but it was consistent with the Fed's objectives. As Reagan had pointed out, the money supply had surged sharply— indeed, by 11.5 percent in December and more than 20 percent in January. Volcker had indicated some puzzlement about this in January; the economy looked too soft for such a big increase. At the time, though, in the interest of preserving the credibility of his anti-inflation fight, tightening seemed the only recourse. Volcker vowed to homebuilders that the central bank had "no intention of letting the money supply get out of control on the upside or the downside."

As the tension between the Fed and the White House mounted, the president and Volcker arranged a peace conference on February 15, at the White House. The two men met alone. Reagan's economic advisors prepared briefing papers urging him to tell Volcker to push for a slow and steady growth in the money supply, but neither would say what was discussed. It was evident, though, that

Volcker had been persuasive. Three days later at a press conference, Reagan had changed his tune. "I have confidence in the announced policies of the Federal Reserve Board," he said. "We also support the Federal Reserve's 1982 money growth targets, which are fully consistent with the administration's projections for the coming year."

Volcker had won this showdown, but it wouldn't be the last. Little did he know that the president, prior to this meeting, had rejected a proposal by supply-side economists that he push for a plan to stabilize interest rates and then move toward a gold standard. Stockman and Regan, in particular, thought this was a dumb idea and persuaded Reagan not to support it. Regan, though, would prove to be a thorn in Volcker's side on more than one occasion in the future.

It was not unusual to see Volcker stand up to such pressure. He always had a fixed idea of where he was going with monetary policy. He would operate within broad parameters, giving here and there, according to how he perceived the political system required accommodation. But he would always keep his eye on the ultimate goal. The approach hinged heavily, of course, on having good information about the course of the economy and his own monetary policy. If something were flawed in that policy, then it would lead to miscalculation and possibly lack of control.

There was something flawed in that policy—and Volcker obviously was aware of it early in 1982. Fred Schultz detected a faint hint of self-doubt in the chairman's mind when the FOMC met on February 1–2, 1982, to consider its monetary targets for the year ahead. Since Schultz's term was expiring and it was to be his last meeting, the chairman granted his request to address the policy-making panel for the last time. Schultz exhorted them, in emphatic words, to stick with the policy, "to hang in there until you have beaten this inflation psychology. I told them that we had to stay the course after going this far. I probably, purposely, made it too strong," he said. "But I had a strong feeling, after I finished, that Paul thought that I had been too strong."

Volcker was a realist and he could spot the trouble coming. With his intuitive sense of markets and his understanding of growing pressures on financial institutions, he anticipated that the Fed would have to back off.

Had the politicians who had lambasted Volcker been listening more closely and with more understanding, they would have discovered that the strongest criticism of the Fed's monetary policy was coming from within the Fed itself. Nancy Teeters, at times a lonely dissenter from Open Market decisions, was saying that the relationship between the money supply and economic growth had broken down and that the Fed was too tight for the country's good. In a speech at Emory University on March 17, 1982, Frank E. Morris, president of the Federal Reserve Bank of Boston said that the pace of financial innovation—with all the new NOW accounts, money market mutual funds, all-savers certificates—had rendered any definition of the money supply "arbitrary and unsatisfactory."

Morris said that any definition of the money supply would include assets that some people view as savings and would exclude other assets that some people would use for immediate transactions. Trying to sort out which was which looked impossible, he said. Morris said the sharp rise in interest rates penalized people who left funds in non-interest-bearing deposits, and thus many rationally put money they intended to use for transactions into accounts drawing interest. Computerization of the financial industry had made it easier and cheaper for banks to keep track of all the new accounts, said Morris.

As for that bulge in the money supply in January, Morris found that most of it had been caused by a buildup in NOW accounts. Yet, on the basis of the surge in the money supply, the Fed had clamped down further in February. Echoing Teeters, Morris said that M1 was no longer a reliable guide to Fed policy because one could not predict how much economic growth each new dollar created would produce. This so-called "velocity" of money had always been hard to predict, but it would be much more so in the future.

From the beginning, Volcker knew about and understood these arguments, even had some sympathy for them. But being technically correct is one thing, and being politically and economically correct is another. Volcker had sold the tight-money policy to the nation and said that he had intended to stick with it until it conquered inflation. For better or worse, the money supply had become the standard by which his policy was measured by the Wall Street financial community, not so much the high level of interest rates and unemployment. To get the country focusing on the money supply rather than interest rates was, after all, his strategy; he could push up interest rates and unemployment without being blamed. Now, to put it bluntly, his options were limited. Even if he wanted to change the Fed's operating procedures, he could not extricate himself from this policy without appearing to lose credibility.

No, the time wasn't ripe yet. Minutes of the FOMC during the first part of 1982 indicated that the central bank was having a difficult time sorting out the monetary numbers. Judging from the discussion, it was torn by the reports of economic hardship building up across the country and the need to stand resolute against an inflation that, while suddenly and dramatically receding, was still perceived as a big danger.

Volcker also worried deeply about the prospect of a financial crisis that would engulf the nation's banking system. He had already had an inkling that Mexico's debt problems could blow up at any time, and with many of the nation's largest banks deeply involved in that country, managing the subsequent crisis could be dicey. The Fed had worked out an arrangement with Mexico—a currency swap—that would provide it with money until perhaps early fall of that year.

In addition, the decline in energy prices, resulting from a worldwide oil glut, had put in jeopardy some banks that lent heavily in the energy industry in the belief that oil prices would continue to rise in the 1980s.

TO BAIL OUT OR NOT TO BAIL OUT?

The first public indication of these simmering troubles in the financial community came on Monday, May 17, when Drysdale Government Securities, a subsidiary of Chase Manhattan Bank, defaulted on a $160 million dollar interest payment. Volcker swung quickly into action when Chase refused to meet its obligations to other Wall Street firms, persuading the bank to make good. Then, a day later, the Fed injected funds into the banking system to allay fears and announced to New York bankers that it stood ready to lend money "to assist commercial banks in meeting unusual credit demands relating to market problems."

Not long after the Drysdale affair settled down, Penn Square Bank in Oklahoma precipitated another crisis. Through bad management, energy loans, aggressive attraction of deposits, and the Fed's tight money, the bank was on the verge of collapse. One of the difficulties was its relationship with other major banks in participating in loans, especially Continental Illinois Bank and Trust Company of Chicago. Continental had been a go-go bank for years as it strove under chairman Roger Anderson's leadership to become one of the top banks in America. Volcker instantly knew one thing: As Penn Square went, so went Continental. If Penn Square collapsed, it would simply be a matter of time before Continental's troubles would erupt.

When Penn Square's difficulties became a matter of public attention in the first week of July, Volcker and the Fed had already been working with banking regulators to try to arrange a solution. The Fed had already lent money to Penn Square, and Volcker's assistants had been trying to work out a plan in which the bank would be merged with another, or there would be a capital infusion, in effect a bailout. In the first few days of July, the banking regulators held a number of meetings to try to decide whether to go for some form of bailout or to let the bank go under, a course favored by free-market regulators led by William Isaac, chairman of the FDIC. The FDIC said it didn't have the authority to bail out the bank, while the Fed contended otherwise. The discussion wound up in a stalemate.

With deep divisions among regulators over what course to pursue, Volcker informed his senior staff on July 4, 1982, a Sunday, that it appeared that Penn Square would collapse. The following day, at a meeting in Volcker's office, the regulators met for the ultimate decision with Treasury Secretary Regan. According to Isaac, Regan asked everyone in the room whether the closure of the bank and the payoff to depositors would disrupt the financial system. Only one spoke up, and that was Volcker. According to Isaac, the Fed chairman raised the prospect of a "substantial chance of financial chaos" if the bank went under. While Volcker did not like bailouts, he felt that the risk of a major financial disruption was too great to take.

To Isaac's surprise, Regan sided with the FDIC chairman. Isaac then went back to his agency to arrange the closing of the bank. As he looked out the window from his office over Washington's major monuments, he began to get second thoughts about his decision. What if Volcker were right? After all, here was a man with great experience and foresight. For a time, Isaac said, he had visions of another Depression with long lines at the nation's banks. Then he got over it quickly and began to work on closing Penn Square.

The closing of Penn Square was another shock to the financial system and another blow to Fed policy. Indeed, fears of another Depression were beginning to spread as the unemployment rate topped 10 percent. Some economists worried that the Fed had clamped down so hard on business activity that easing up might not do the job. The analogy was that it would be somewhat like trying to push on a string, with income so depressed.

"By summer, an atmosphere of gloom and depression was present at the Fed," said board governor Lyle Gramley. "The Fed was in quite a quandary." In the previous year or so, he said, the central bank had tried to steer a middle course through the muddle created by NOW accounts and the erratic behavior of the money supply. In mid-1982, with the unemployment rate above 10 percent, bankruptcies rising, and banks failing, the time had come for serious reassessment. "The question was whether we would pay less attention to what happened to the money supply and more to what was happening to the real economy. The decision-making process at the Fed was flawed, but in an innocent way." By that, he meant that the reliance on the 1979 monetarist policy had probably been excessive. The time to back off was nearing, but it had to be done with finesse.

In addition, said Gramley, the summer of 1982 provided evidence that something had to be done to get the international economy moving up again.

INFLATION TURNS THE CORNER . . .
AND MORE TROUBLES AWAIT

Volcker had already given a signal on May 21 in Chicago that the measurement of money was off the mark and that the central bank would feel all right in overshooting the M1 target. Under the same circumstances in February, of course, the Fed had tightened almost routinely. Volcker blamed technical reasons for the switch in attitude— meaning the big rise in NOW accounts.

At the next FOMC meeting, which occurred during the debate over the closing of Penn Square, the Fed decided to ease slightly and said that it would permit the money supply to rise outside its targeted ranges if financial problems warranted. It was not a major backing off of the targets, however, because Volcker went to Congress on July 20 to reaffirm them. It was one of his more rugged congressional appearances, as members of the Senate Banking Committee greeted him with a barrage of criticism over high interest rates. Senator Paul S. Sarbanes (D., Maryland) called the Fed's policy a failure and said Volcker could cut interest rates and lower unemployment without compromising the Fed's fight against inflation. "The economy seems to be on a disastrous course," Senator Donald W. Riegle, Jr. (D., Michigan), told Volcker. "The situation is at a desperate point."

Significantly, Volcker declared: "The evidence now seems to be strong that the inflationary tide has turned in a fundamental way."

It was his first declaration in three years that his policy finally had turned the corner and was succeeding. Indeed, the figures backed him up. Consumer prices rose at an annual rate of 5.7 percent in the first half of 1982, and they were that high only because of big bulges in May and June that would not be repeated later. Another inflation measurement, the GNP's implicit price deflator, showed prices rising by 5 percent in the first half of the year.

In spite of this, Volcker was deeply worried. Although the economy had improved in the second quarter, it was still obviously in recession. The financial strains were still present.

In mid-August, Volcker went on a fishing trip to Jackson, Wyoming, along with Gerald Corrigan, then the president of the Minneapolis Federal Reserve Bank, and Ed Yeo, a partner at Morgan Stanley and an old friend. As he fished for trout on the banks of the Snake River with hs friends, Volcker enjoyed the respite from the travails in Washington.

The first thing to disturb their serenity was the sight of Roger Anderson, chairman of Continental Illinois National Bank and Trust Company. He had flown to Jackson in his corporate jet and arrived with a camera around his neck and worry in his heart. "I knew we were in trouble when I saw that Roger had a suit and tie on," said Yeo.

Volcker and Anderson sat on the front porch of the cabin along the Snake River, with the Grand Tetons in the background, discussing the troubles of Continental. The banker was seeking moral support and, perhaps down the road, monetary support as well. He was going off to New York to speak with bankers there. There was little that Volcker could do immediately but hold Anderson's hand and encourage him to work on the bank's problems.

It was clear, however, that Continental's problems would be high in Volcker's mind for the next two years, when it finally would be rescued by the FDIC, with the help of a direct loan from Volcker's agency.

The next thing to jar Volcker's trip was a telephone call that Mexico was broke and unable to make payments on its loans. Citibank, Chase Manhattan, the Bank of America, and Manufacturers Hanover all had heavy exposure in Mexico, and an actual default could plunge the United States into a major financial crisis.

In one day, Volcker had been given enough evidence to persuade him it was time to seek a way to extricate the Fed from its monetary policy. The Third World debt crisis had dawned. Was there a banking crisis to follow? Volcker packed his gear and was off to Washington as soon as he could get out.

The Mexican announcement had caught the Reagan administration and Regan's Treasury off guard. Contingency plans had been developed, said Beryl Sprinkel, undersecretary of monetary affairs, but the entire problem had not been given the serious attention it deserved. When Mexico made its announcement, it genuinely surprised Regan, according to those familiar with the situation. "It should have been no surprise to them," one Fed aide noted. "We had been tearing our hair out over Mexico for months and months and months." Volcker had hoped that the Fed's swapline assistance, in which foreign currencies are exchanged, would tide Mexico over longer.

Through this crisis, the White House gained a greater appreciation of Volcker's talents, said former Reagan aide Rich Williamson.

The Mexican situation sobered the Fed even more. With inflation easing, the recession still lingering, and the money supply no longer reflecting real economic conditions, the time for ending the experiment voted on October 6, 1979, was near. Volcker was frustrated. He wanted a recovery badly. When the money supply had briefly fallen within Fed targets in the summer it had eased. But now, the money supply was rising beyond the targets again, putting the pressure on for a tightening. "The jig was up," Volcker said.

It was October 5, 1982, to be exact, when the Fed decided it would not have a target for M1 for the rest of the year. It cited the growth in NOW accounts and all-savers certificates, which had distorted the money supply. But the real reason, as Volcker knew, was Mexico and the threat of an international debt crisis that could plunge the world into a much deeper recession than the one under way.

Steven Axilrod, a top Fed aide, said that Volcker made two key decisions—the one to start the monetarist experiment in 1979 and, possibly greater, to extricate the Fed from it three years in the future. The Fed would, for a time, still pay attention to the money targets, but after the October 5 decision, it would be less monetarist than before. It would not slavishly make decisions based on rises and falls in the money supply, which it had before.

Volcker announced the easing on October 9 at Hot Springs, Virginia, where he spoke to the prestigious Business Council. He spoke of the monetary distortions and the apparent breakdown between M1 growth and GNP. This, too, was a new Volcker in another sense. It was his attitude. It was upbeat, not sober.

"Let me say I am encouraged," he said, "I think the inflationary momentum that had come to grip the economy in the '60s and '70s has been broken. None of us has any feeling that concern of monetary policy—that continuing concern about inflation—is something that can be turned on and off."

Paul Volcker had done it. Inflation as measured by the consumer price index rose 3.9 percent in 1982. He got a lot of help from the collapse of OPEC, of course, and assistance from a stronger dollar. Inflation would continue to remain under control for the next several years even as the economy began to recover and unemployment finally began to decline.

But his worries were far from over. The deficit, partly because of the recession, was getting worse, not better. Suddenly the U.S. began to import massive amounts of foreign capital, lured by high interest rates. It would not be long before the trade balance would go into deep deficit. Yes, inflation had been conquered, but as every good economist understands, anything worth having has a price.

10

"NINJA"
AND THE DEATH
OF BRETTON WOODS

Late in 1968, Bob Roosa had some powerful companions when he rode in the club car of the New Haven Railroad to work in New York City. One was Charls Walker, a Texan and an economist who had known Volcker for a long time. The other was John Mitchell, a confidant to President-elect Richard M. Nixon and later attorney general.

Walker had connections in the Republican Party and in the economic community and was destined to become a key official in the new administration. Mitchell was, according to Roosa, deeply involved in personnel selection for the new Nixon administration.

"We talked about who should be the secretary of the treasury," Roosa said. "Walter Wriston [of Citibank] had turned it down. I suggested Dave Kennedy [a Chicago banker]. He said that Walker was going to be the deputy secretary. The obvious question was: Who was going to be the undersecretary for monetary affairs? That's when I began planting Volcker's name with Mitchell."

Walker remembers those club car rides but doesn't know whether that was what clinched the job for Volcker in the new administration. It clearly did not hurt, however. He said he had known Volcker for a long time and recommended him for the post. Walker's first remembrance of Volcker was in New York in 1954, when as a young economist in the Federal Reserve Bank of Texas, he came to visit the New York Fed. There he saw Volcker working on the trading desk.

The fact that Volcker was a nominal Democrat and had worked in a Democratic administration did not disqualify him from a high post in the Nixon Treasury. He came highly recommended from his work with Rockefeller and for an economic philosophy that traditional Republicans like Walker felt extremely comfortable with. He had impressed others with good economic credentials when he came to Washington for work on several advisory committees late in the 1960s. Volcker jumped at the job. He felt that he was stuck in his position at Chase and was overqualified in a sense after his previous work at the Treasury. His new post, undersecretary of monetary affairs, had suddenly become one of the most important in Washington. The undersecretary's job encompassed the whole international monetary arena, government debt, and domestic monetary policy. Walker, as deputy secretary, would leave most of the international work to Volcker. The new secretary, David M. Kennedy, was well versed in international economics, but he did not have the same breadth of experience as Volcker.

It was Walker who went to New York and asked Volcker to take the job. Walker said he and Kennedy had discussed possible candidates, and "Volcker was head and shoulders above them all." It was obvious as soon as the new administration took office in 1969 that the winds of change were sweeping across the world economy. The postwar monetary system had started to come under increasing attack as a consequence of the United States' persistent balance-of-payments deficit. George P. Shultz, who later was to become Volcker's boss at Treasury and still later secretary of state under Ronald Reagan, said that this situation began after World War II when the U.S. began providing dollars to a dollar-hungry world in the form of foreign aid and loans. The dollar shortage disappeared in the 1950s, and the U.S. began losing gold as other countries converted excess currency, Shultz noted. "A series of palliatives followed, one upon another, throughout the 1960s as the government tried to deal with the consequences of what by then had become an overvalued dollar, held at a value above its free-market price by the U.S. commitment to exchange the dollar for gold at $35 an ounce," Shultz wrote in a book, *Economic Policy Beyond the Headlines*, coauthored by Kenneth Dam.

One of those palliatives was the interest equalization tax that Volcker wrote on Roosa's behalf, and another was the creation of paper gold, the international reserve asset that was designed to permit the U.S. to hold its gold when other nations came calling with surplus currency to convert. Called *special drawing rights*, all it did was supplement the role of gold. Over the 1960s, the monetary system jumped from crisis to crisis, and governments tried move after move, mostly of a patchwork fashion, to respond to them.

THE BEGINNING OF THE END FOR BRETTON WOODS

Nixon knew in 1968 that the international monetary system could be a problem if he were elected president; that was evident from the recurring crises. In the fall campaign, he chose the silver-haired and scholarly economist Arthur F. Burns for a unique mission. Burns had served as President Eisenhower's chief economic advisor and head of the influential Bureau of Economic Research and would later become a White House counselor and chairman of the Federal Reserve Board.

"I went on a secret mission for Richard Nixon to test

European opinion on the issue of raising the price of gold," Burns said. "I went about it very discreetly. I gave no indication to anyone, first, that I was Nixon's emissary and, second, that he or I had anything like that in mind. I came to the definite conclusion that this would be accepted by Europeans. I recommended prompt action right after the election [to raise the price of gold]. I did that on a plane trip with Nixon during the campaign. The poor man had his mind on the speech and on the election and then probably forgot about it. In any case, he did nothing about it. And that was the time to do it, right after the election."

Raising the price of gold would have amounted to a unilateral devaluation of the dollar, hardly the type of action that signifies strength for a new administration. A fresh administration would have thought twice about that, even if the dollar was overvalued and action was clearly needed. The new Treasury secretary, David Kennedy, was not noted for boldness of action, and his chief monetary man, forty-one-year-old Paul Volcker, was not prepared to accept devaluation quite so soon.

Neither was Volcker impressed with proposals to make the monetary system more flexible by allowing exchange rates for currencies to fluctuate more widely. This had, after all, been the principal problem with the system developed at Bretton Woods, New Hampshire, in the waning years of World War II. It permitted currency values to rise and fall within a narrow band. If a nation could not maintain this value on the upside or downside, it had to revalue and devalue its currency. All currencies were valued in terms of the dollar, and the dollar itself was set at $35 an ounce of gold, making gold the center of the system. Critics said this system, while requiring great discipline from countries to correct their domestic economic policies, had just become too rigid.

On his first trip to Europe after being named under-secretary, Volcker encountered a question about whether the values of currencies should be permitted to fluctuate more widely. "These ideas have had a lot of discussion in academic circles, and that's where they can stay," he said. Volcker also showed that, as a Treasury official, he didn't mind telling the Federal Reserve what it should be doing. The number one objective in the U.S. at the time was to regain control of inflation, and "if that means restrictive monetary policies, so be it," said Volcker.

Volcker has one vivid recollection of that first trip overseas as undersecretary, held in conjunction with a meeting of the Organization for Economic Cooperation and Development. Afterward, he said, the heads of the various delegations gathered for a secret dinner meeting at the home of the Dutch ambassador in Paris. "We were in the dying throes of the Bretton Woods system, and these were the people who supported it," Volcker noted. "I still remember one of the officials wagging his finger at me and saying, 'You'd better be careful what you are saying, or else you will bring down the entire monetary system.'"

It took two more years for the Bretton Woods system to collapse, but it wasn't anything that Volcker said. It was inevitable. As Shultz noted, overvaluation of the dollar meant that imports began pouring into the United States. The nation's trading partners were delighted at their good fortune on this score, but soon their official holdings of dollars escalated. These dollar holdings by foreign central banks grew from $23.8 billion at the end of 1970 to $36.2 billion by July 30, 1971, roughly three times the value of American gold holdings. It dawned on Volcker and other top officials that the Treasury's gold holdings could be wiped out in a crisis.

A NEW PLAN: WAGE-PRICE FREEZE, IMPORT SURCHARGE . . .

Nixon became impatient with his administrations's economic policy. Inflation had "soared" to an annual rate of nearly 6 percent in mid-1971, and unemployment also was in the 6 percent range. While these rates were low, compared with what was to follow later, the U.S. had never before encountered such a double dose of economic problems during the postwar era.

The president was looking for decisiveness, and he did not see it in the economic team he had chosen for his administration. Kennedy at Treasury was cautious, and so was his Council of Economic Advisers. Nixon made a fateful decision, appointing John B. Connally, the flamboyant former Texas governor, as Treasury secretary in the spring of 1971.

Soon after, under Connally's orders, Volcker was working on a new economic plan, one that would feature a wage-price freeze and the end of the Bretton Woods monetary system. The latter would be accomplished by ending the U.S. commitment to convert foreign dollar holdings into gold. The program, especially wage-price controls, went against the philosophy of many of Nixon's conservative advisors, but by now Connally clearly had Nixon's ear on economics. The Texan favored tough action to tackle the domestic inflation and to put foreign countries in their place with a tough new international economic policy.

Volcker's pragmatism came to the fore. Although he preferred tighter money to control inflation, he went along with the wage-price freeze proposal and even worked on it closely with Murray Weidenbaum, the Treasury's top domestic economist and Volcker's subordinate. Weidenbaum had become extremely impatient with the administration's refusal to call for any marketplace restraint on rising prices and began working on the freeze idea with Volcker's permission. The business community, oddly enough, began to be supportive of strong government action to fight inflation. Arthur Burns himself had been enamored of a government wage-price council.

"There was a lot of public discussion about a price freeze," Volcker said. "I thought that was a pretty good idea. You kind of gave inflation a temporary kill. It sounded just like the kind of thing that Brazil and Argentina and others were doing. I thought it would be a three-month thing to be backed by sufficiently stern monetary and fiscal policy." But Volcker discovered that his hope for a quick freeze, to be followed by stringent monetary and fiscal policy, was naive. An elaborate wage-price control system followed, and it took three years to dismantle it. Volcker said he was appalled in 1971 when he learned that this was to be the plan.

Volcker found that he was constantly having to block tough proposals coming from Connally, including trade restrictions of various kinds that would have surely started a trade war if they had been adopted. To his credit, Connally usually listened to reason, except on the issue of the import surcharge. The secretary assigned Volcker to do the staff work on a 10 percent surcharge on imports, an idea to which Volcker strenuously objected. He thought that he could talk the secretary out of it and kept delaying the staff workup, but Connally kept pushing, and Volcker finally relented. Others in the administration liked the idea of the import surcharge because of its dramatic, attention-getting nature. It was meant to be temporary, but it would serve as a bargaining chip in the more important work, realigning the major currencies of the world. To the Japanese, the import surcharge was a virtual declaration of economic war.

Connally's Treasury was working furiously on all these ideas in the spring and early summer of 1971, with Volcker the key staff man. Herbert Stein, chairman of the Council of Economic Advisers, said that Nixon and Connally had decided in the spring to close the gold window if foreign demands for gold became so strong and, additionally, to impose wage-price controls. According to George Shultz, who at the time was director of the Office of Management and Budget, it was Connally who persuaded Nixon to adopt an "integrated" economic strategy to deal with rising prices and the dollar. Nixon decided to go with the plan after two meetings with his top economic advisors in the old executive office building. It was decided that the announcement would be made in September, after Labor

Day, because Nixon wanted to consult with Congress, but it was summer, and Congress was in recess.

Shultz said that after the decision was made his twelve-year-old son, who saved almost every penny he made, heard a discussion over the radio about dollar devaluation and asked his father what that meant. After his father explained, Shultz's son said, "Well, Dad, I almost wanted my money to be worth more."

"When I told Nixon that story the following Monday, it scared the living bejesus out of him," Shultz said. "He didn't want to be the president who devalued the dollar, but of course he could see what was happening."

. . . AND CLOSING THE GOLD WINDOW

August in Washington is usually a dead month. Congress leaves on recess, and the bureaucracy shrinks down to a shadow of its former self as people stream out of the city on vacation. August 1971 began that way. Connally was one of those who went on vacation, looking ahead to a lively September. But there was trouble. On August 12, a Thursday, the British government came to the U.S. Treasury and asked for $9 billion in gold. That stunned Volcker.

"I was around," said Shultz. "The director of the budget is always around. I remember that Paul Volcker came to see me. The gist of his message was that the demands for gold were coming, he thought, at such a rate that our hand was forced and that we must close the gold window, or this ridiculous price would wipe out our gold supply. It was getting to be a run on it, so there wasn't an alternative. So we went to Nixon and said, 'Time has run out. We have to do this, and we have to do it this weekend.' "

What followed was one of the most remarkable economic decisions in American history. Nixon's top advisors were helicoptered to the mountaintop presidential retreat in Camp David, Maryland, on Friday the 13th. Shultz said it was decided the group would be self-contained and would not have to be in touch with the outside world in order to make a decision. Thus, Volcker, who had done most of the key staff work on the international economic measures, went along.

As chronicled by then White House advisor William Safire, Nixon gathered his advisors in Camp David's Aspen Cottage Friday afternoon for a five-hour discussion on the economics and politics of the history-making plan. Connally stressed the boldness of the plan and pushed hard for the import surcharge as a bargaining chip to induce other countries to realign their exchange rates. Burns, who had by now become the chairman of the Fed after serving as a White House economic advisor, urged against closing the gold window. He thought that the impact of the president's other measures would renew confidence in the dollar and halt the gold drain.

Volcker was reluctant, but he knew there was no other choice. "I hate to do this, to close the gold window," he told the group. "All my life I have defended exchange rates, but I think it is needed." He said also the administration should waste no time in trying to negotiate a new regime of exchange rates with its allies. Further, Volcker said, the U.S. ought to consider deemphasizing the role of gold in the monetary system and perhaps even sell some of it. But his effort to introduce international monetary reform at Camp David failed; Nixon and the other participants wanted none of it.

Years later, Volcker said closing the gold window had not turned out as he wanted. "I wanted to do it. I had written all the papers to justify doing it. I was in an advocacy position, but it was a very regretful advocacy position. I thought that we would get the [monetary system] put back together again as soon as we could. At Camp David, the focus was not on what was going to happen two months from now; it was on how it was going to be presented. So all the ideas I had about how we would convene meetings and consider ideas about monetary reform were never looked at."

There were two principal reasons, in Volcker's view. Shultz, who was schooled in the free-market, monetarist school of Milton Friedman, did not believe in fixed exchange rates of currencies; he thought the market could do the job of balancing out currency values. Connally, on the other hand, was not a long-term thinker; his aim was to use the closing of the gold window and the import surcharge to achieve the immediate political goal, obtaining a realignment of exchange rates and ending the overvaluation of the dollar.

THE SMITHSONIAN AGREEMENT

On August 15, 1971, President Nixon went on national television and electrified the country by announcing a 90-day wage-price freeze, a 10 percent import surcharge, and the closing of the gold window. All three were to be temporary and to be followed in Nixon's mind by stable prices and a stable dollar. He said he wanted to put to rest the "bugaboo" of devaluation, although ending the overvaluation of the dollar was clearly the administration's goal.

Unhinging the dollar from gold effectively ended the Bretton Woods system and sent Volcker into a flurry of activity, speaking with finance ministers and their deputies on a realignment of exchange rates. As Shultz wrote, the import surcharge was an effective "signal" that the U.S. wanted the exchange rates changed. "Secretary Connally flashed the signal in true Texas style, with both guns blazing in the corridors of international finance," Shultz wrote. "He did gain the attention of foreign governments at the highest level and used the surcharge effectively in negotiations. It was withdrawn when a new set of exchange relationships, resulting in a devaluation of the dollar in terms of gold of 7.9 percent, was agreed upon at the Smithsonian Institution in December 1971."

Immediately after the August decision, Volcker went overseas to speak with finance ministers and deal with the consequent turmoil. In Japan, they called his boss "Typhoon" Connally because of the surcharge and his insistence that other countries share in the cost of American defense. In several meetings in the fall of 1971, the U.S. resisted raising the price of gold, insisting that other countries change their currencies instead. But negotiations were difficult; other countries didn't want to revalue their currencies significantly.

The breakthrough came at a meeting of the finance ministers of the top ten industrial countries in Rome on December 1. Volcker raised a hypothetical case. If the U.S. decided to devalue by 10 to 15 percent, what would the other countries do? he asked. Connally picked up Volcker's theme. There was a long silence, and then the other delegates indicated they would follow as long as the U.S. was willing to make a contribution. Two weeks later, at a meeting in the Azores, Nixon and French President Georges Pompidou reached agreement on a plan that would include devaluation of the dollar.

This led to the famed Smithsonian agreement of December 17, 1971, a new currency realignment that would call for raising the price of gold to $38 an ounce. According to Federal Reserve official Robert Solomon, Connally, Burns, and Volcker skillfully wheedled the other ministers into a maximum revaluation of their currencies in relation to the dollar. Volcker distributed a table calling for a 9 percent dollar devaluation, but that was scaled back to 7.9 percent, he noted.

When it was over, they called for the president. Standing beneath the famed Wright Brothers airplane, Nixon announced the new deal as "the most significant monetary agreement in the history of the world."

It was far from that. The gold window remained closed, and the currency realignment did not really reflect the economic strength of the countries. The dollar was pegged at too high a rate. The most important thing was that the U.S. and other governments had let valuable time slip by in trying to reform the monetary system. The Smithsonian deal, however, was a feather in Volcker's cap. Along with Connally, he had shown good negotiating skills and gained the respect of some key officials in foreign countries who would later become heads of state—including Valery Giscard d'Estaing of France and Helmut Schmidt of West Germany. This goodwill abroad would help Volcker immensely when he took over as Federal Reserve chief.

Volcker was a good friend of Arthur F. Burns, the Fed chairman, but he disagreed with Burns's monetary policy during this critical period. Had Burns decided to adopt a restrictive monetary policy, Volcker thought, it would have helped defuse the monetary crises and inflation problems that pounded the Nixon administration despite the wage-price controls he had put into effect. During the first six months of 1971, when the dollar crisis became the most acute, the money supply expanded at an annual rate of almost 10 percent, contributing to rising prices and less confidence in the dollar. The next year, an election year, the money supply rose 7.4 percent, building up more inflationary pressures even as it helped Nixon get reelected.

Burns had spent the better part of his post-Fed career defending himself against the charge that he was too loose and responded too freely to White House pressure. He said he had to balance fighting rising unemployment with fighting inflation. He could have said that the political system of that time would have come down on the Fed's head if he had squeezed money tighter. In 1970, when Burns was a little more restrictive, Nixon and the White House staff were constantly badgering him, to the point that Burns took to lecturing the president for interfering with the Fed. Oddly enough in those days, when Burns was conducting a relatively loose monetary policy, the financial press was writing about his tight-money policies.

After being told that he would not be Nixon's running mate or secretary of state, Connally left the Nixon administration in May 1972, and George Shultz was named to replace him. Shultz, a strong, quiet man who worked well behind the scenes, did not have his heart in monetary reform as did Volcker, but he could not ignore the demands for some new plan for reshaping the system that were emanating from the nation's allies.

Connally came in to see Volcker and say good-bye. "We've had a lot of good times together and a lot of battles, and you've won most of them," he told Volcker, who delights in telling the story because of the many off-the-wall ideas he had beaten back. The dashing Connally style in many respects rubbed off on Volcker. More than one person noticed it. From the Texan, Volcker learned wheeling and dealing and how to thrive in the spotlight. He grew under Connally, who liked and respected him.

Burns had caught the Treasury off guard when he made a speech in Montreal in May outlining ten elements necessary to a reformed monetary system. The irony is that Volcker, who was later to take Burns's position at the Fed, found it necessary to criticize Burns for speaking out of school. He said Burns wasn't speaking for the government and added "we haven't any prepackaged plan for reform to spring on the waiting world, nor, frankly, have we found other nations ready to pronounce their considered judgments."

Shultz, though, saw the need for the U.S. to make a monetary proposal to meet the objections from abroad. Shultz and a team of other top officials from other agencies met in the library of the White House to develop the plan. All that committee work, however, could not match Volcker's mind. Volcker sketched out the plan largely on his own, and Shultz adopted it. It became known as the "Volcker plan" even though Shultz outlined it at the annual meeting of the International Monetary Fund and World Bank in the fall of 1972.

Shultz deserves the credit for putting the idea forward, but his little library group didn't do the real thinking. Another Treasury official, Jack Bennett, had been assigned to develop a monetary reform plan with the help of officials from other agencies. As Solomon wrote in his book, *The International Monetary System, 1945–1976*:

> While the interagency group under Jack Bennett had been arguing and floundering, Paul Volcker sat in his office and pieced together an integrated proposal for a reformed monetary system. He had it in a form sufficiently complete to try out on others in the government in August, and I was called back from a Cape Cod vacation to work on the plan with a small group from other agencies. My files identify it as Plan X.

It got to the heart of the problem with other countries: countries with a balance of payments surplus felt less pressure to change the value of their currencies than those in deficit. If the world was ever going to get back to a system with a relatively fixed value for currencies, some mechanism was needed to solve this problem.

Volcker's idea was to put pressure on countries whose economies were performing well to increase the value of their currencies, just as a nation with a balance of payments surplus would be under pressure to devalue its currency. The basic guidepost was to be how much reserves—such as foreign currencies and gold—a country accumulated. If a rich country built up reserves by keeping its currency undervalued and exporting around the world (e.g., Japan), it would be expected to revalue its currency upward.

The Volcker plan was well received internationally when it was announced at the annual International Monetary Fund/World Bank meetings, but it was clear that other countries had many points of division. France was seeking a return to a system based on gold. West Germany worried about the explosion of international capital and whether that would overwhelm any system of relatively fixed exchange rates. (The Volcker plan had remarkable similarities to an economic proposal announced in 1986 by Treasury Secretary James A. Baker III. Both plans stressed the use of objective economic indicators to force action and increased coordination among the major industrial countries. In some key respects the Baker plan of 1986— adopted at the Tokyo economic summit—was a dusted-off version of the 1972 Volcker plan.) But monetary reform died not long after it was presented because of some extraordinary economic shocks.

'ROUND THE WORLD IN FIVE DAYS

On January 11, 1973, Shultz—who never liked the wage-price controls—announced that the mandatory Phase 2 was ending and a largely voluntary Phase 3 was beginning. Volcker thought that the move was ill-timed. It came when the dollar had dropped to low levels, boosting inflationary pressures. And Burns's efforts at the Fed appeared toothless. Suddenly, the U.S. was in the middle of another international economic crisis. In February 1973, the administration saw the need for another realignment of exchange rates, even if it meant a devaluation of the dollar. Shultz this time sent Volcker on a 'round-the-world mission to handle the negotiations single-handedly. In addition, it was anticipated that this would be the last realignment; exchange rates would be stabilized through a reform plan immediately following.

Volcker testified before Congress the morning of February 12 and then immediately went to the airport en route to Tokyo. No one told the Japanese he was coming until the plane was in the air.

"I very much wanted to do this thing," he said. "The idea was that we would devalue once more, and then we would try to stabilize things. Let's get this thing settled once and for all. We devalue and then stabilize it. That was the plan. The deal in my mind was very clear. We'd devalue, the Japanese would revalue, and the Europeans would stand still."

A six-foot-seven Volcker amid much smaller Japanese might be easy to spot, but he managed to escape attention. He drove to the home of Japanese Finance Minister Takeo Fukuda and, after several hours of negotiation, discovered that the Japanese would be willing to let the yen float upward by 10 percent if the U.S. devalued. "This was a remarkable thing for the Japanese to do," Volcker said. Although it wasn't an agreement for an outright upward revaluation, it was close to that.

When Volcker left the minister's residence, he left his hat behind, and, for a time, that worried the Japanese, who were afraid that somehow his trip to Tokyo might be discovered. Nevertheless, Volcker returned to the airport in Tokyo in hopes of taking off immediately for Bonn. He was told by the crew that they couldn't leave because of rules requiring eight hours of rest. "This wasn't in the plan," Volcker said. "We hadn't allowed for eight hours of rest. We had to get that countermanded by the secretary of defense, which took an hour or so."

Volcker's plane flew over the pole, the shortest route to Bonn, but it wasn't short enough. When he heard Volcker was coming, West German Finance Minister Schmidt intuitively knew what the trip was about and took a plane to Paris, where he could confer with Giscard d'Estaing to get a unified position. Volcker said that, as his plane was landing on one end of the runway, Schmidt's was taking off at the other. Schmidt and Giscard favored a European solution, permitting European currencies to float against the dollar and yen, not the Volcker plan. The British chancellor of the exchequer, Anthony Barber, killed this idea, however. The British still had not pegged the pound to Common Market countries and weren't ready to do so.

Volcker finally met with Schmidt when the West German finance minister returned, and then he was off to London, then to Paris and Rome, negotiating all the way. Although he wanted the devaluation plan, he was, according to several involved, willing to accept a joint float, too.

Finally, French President Georges Pompidou told Giscard that France would accept the devaluation if other Common Market countries would accept it. A tired Volcker arrived back in Paris and was invited to Giscard's official apartment at midnight, where he was told that West Germany, Great Britain, France, and Italy had agreed to the U.S. devaluation if Japan would accept some revaluation.

The deal was struck in five long, weary days reminiscent of Henry Kissinger's shuttle diplomacy. Volcker's daughter, Janice, had joined him toward the end of the trip. He still remembers a photograph of himself and Janice in a French newspaper, *L'Express*. "They were very bitter about this devaluation," said Volcker. "I'll never forget the caption. 'Mr. Volcker, the personification of American imperialism, rode through Paris with his daughter as if he were on vacation.' "

When Volcker returned to Washington six days after his odyssey began, his biological clock was all mixed up. He thought it was Wednesday, when it was actually Tuesday. For his stealth, Fukuda would nickname him "Ninja," after the Japanese warrior class noted for its devotion to the element of surprise.

"Ninja" had gained fame by slipping in and slipping out, but his work didn't last. It didn't last much more than a month, in fact. As Shultz noted, 1973 was a year of rapidly rising inflation on a worldwide scale, and that contributed to a further unraveling of the current regime of currency values. U.S. allies began arguing over when and how they would support these new currency rates through formal intervention. This gave Shultz the opening he had long sought, which was to go to a regime of floating exchange rates for the long term. At a mid-March meeting in Paris, he sat silently as his fellow finance ministers began to argue for floating rates as the only feasible alternative. At the crucial moment, when others had come around to his point of view, he said something to the effect of "I think the U.S. can live with that."

It was done. The ministers agreed that they would intervene only to maintain "orderly" markets but not to defend any particular exchange rate.

Volcker's thin hopes of returning to a more stable monetary system rested with a newly formed panel of the International Monetary Fund called the Committee of 20. The committee set "fixed but adjustable exchange rates" as a goal but never could come up with an acceptable plan.

Volcker pressed his case at Committee of 20 meetings. He indicated that he had little sympathy for the IMF's powers to force countries to adjust their undervalued or overvalued currencies through consultation. The IMF did not treat countries uniformly when disagreements arose. If the country was small, Volcker said, it fell in line with the IMF. If it was large, the IMF fell into line. If several countries disagreed with the IMF, the IMF disappeared, he said.

REFORM YIELDS TO A FLOATING-RATE SYSTEM

Monetary reform died in 1973 with the outbreak of the Arab-Israeli war in October. That led to the Arab oil embargo and the quadrupling of oil prices with the formation of OPEC. With turmoil like this in the monetary markets, Shultz said a flexible floating-rate system was highly desirable. There were a few more stabs at monetary reform in 1974, but for all practical purposes it was over. The IMF ratified the floating-rate system formally at a meeting in Jamaica early in 1976.

Volcker felt frustrated that he was unable to restore some of the stability associated with the old Bretton Woods system. But it was not the last time he would have influence in this area. He helped Treasury Secretary James A. Baker III put together a plan for economic coordination among the industrial countries that was adopted at the Tokyo summit in 1986. In the monetary turbulence of the late 1980s, he said, the world is groping for a return to a system that calls for stable exchange rates.

The floating-rate system was far from perfect. It did not guarantee the type of automatic adjustments in exchange rates that normally would have been expected. For instance, the dollar was overvalued in President Reagan's first term, largely because of high interest rates generated by the budget deficit and tight money. The floating system also lacks discipline. A nation that is duty-bound to defend a specific exchange rate for its currency is careful about having irresponsible fiscal and monetary policies that would undermine it.

A BRIEF SABBATICAL AND BACK TO THE BIG APPLE

Volcker left the Treasury in 1974 as Nixon's presidency was unraveling and joined the Woodrow Wilson School at Princeton, his alma mater. There he spent a year teaching and reflecting, but it was primarily a parking place for a year. He had already been told that he would become president of the New York Federal Reserve Bank when Alfred Hayes retired the following year.

Once again, a mentor assisted Volcker. This time it wasn't Roosa, but Burns, who in those days ran the Federal Reserve System with an iron hand. "It was by far our most important bank," said Burns. "I wanted someone who was an expert in the monetary and banking area—a man of good character. I wanted someone whom I knew personally and therefore I could trust. His name occurred to me rather promptly. In my own mind, there were no competitors. He and I had worked together when he was undersecretary of monetary affairs. He and I differed frequently, but we were able to talk over our differences."

On August 1, 1975, Volcker took over as president of the New York Fed, returning to the place where he had landed his first full-time job. He and his wife bought an apartment on East 79th Street and Lexington Avenue in New York.

Until Jimmy Carter called him in 1979, Volcker was happy in his work, handling the affairs of the biggest Fed bank and participating in monetary policy in Washington as a member of the FOMC.

From his votes on the FOMC, he indicated that he favored a more restrictive policy than the Fed had pursued throughout the 1970s, especially when William Miller succeeded Arthur Burns as chairman.

Volcker also played a direct role in dollar-rescue operations. James McGroarty, now a top official at Discount Corporation of New York, recalls when he worked on the international side of the trading desk that Volcker often would show up in the trading room and watch the action. "He would call into the trading room quite frequently," McGroarty said. On November 1, 1978, McGroarty reported for work at 7:00 A.M. There, sitting in front of the computers watching the action in money markets, was Volcker. "I said, 'Something's up,' " and it was. President Carter had announced a dollar-rescue plan that morning, and Volcker was there to oversee foreign-exchange operations of the Fed in New York.

"Ninja" just couldn't help himself. He had to be part of the action.

11
SOUTH OF THE BORDER, SEND MONEY OUR WAY

Friday, August 13, 1982, was hot and steamy in Washington, DC, a fitting day to launch an international crisis. Volcker had just returned from his Wyoming fishing trip and settled down for a visit from the Mexican delegation, headed by Jesus (Chucho) Silva-Herzog, the minister of finance.

Volcker was not at all surprised that the debt problem was now mushrooming into a crisis. He had seen it coming for more than a year and a half. Indeed, not long after he took office, he began a private campaign to try to curtail the surge of bank lending in the Third World. He knew that banks were becoming overextended, but his efforts were rebuffed. The banks told the Federal Reserve to get lost. There was too much money to make.

The leader among American bankers in this regard was Walter B. Wriston, the flinty chairman of Citicorp. Wriston believed that sovereign nations do not go bankrupt. He had made this point over and over to the Fed. American bankers were like lemmings in those days. They tended to follow the big boys like Wriston; where he saw profit, they saw it, too. Volcker understood the psychology well because he had been director of forward planning at Chase Manhattan. Forward planning at Chase, he would tell friends, was doing what Citicorp did yesterday.

"Paul felt that Wriston led the whole kit and kaboodle up the primrose path," said one person close to the chairman's thinking. "Walt's idea that a country never defaults played a big role in Don Regan's thinking. They were surging blindly ahead and taking a whole bunch of people with them. Volcker had a different philosophy on what a banker ought to do. It was pretty conventional: bankers take other people's money, and they should take care of it."

But the opposite was happening, and Volcker saw a certain profligacy in this. In 1981, banks lent to Mexico at a giddy pace. There was still the belief that, despite Volcker's efforts, inflation would remain high. There were huge parties every time a New York bank lent $1 billion or more to Mexico or another Third World debtor. Even when someone tried to talk sense into the bankers, reminding them that Volcker's tight money might cause a day of reckoning, the bankers plunged ahead. Mexico, too, believed that, with its oil discoveries, its future was bright. In 1981, Mexico borrowed $21 billion. By 1982, it owed $80 billion. The nine largest U.S. banks had 44 percent of their capital tied up in Mexican debt; for the 15 largest regional banks, the figure was 35 percent of their capital.

It was against this background that Volcker confronted Silva-Herzog, a personable, witty man, in his office on Friday the 13th. Chucho had a straightforward message: Mexico could not pay its debts. The $700 million it had borrowed via currency swaps, in effect a credit line, on August 4 had been spent. This was only one of several Mexican borrowings of this kind since May, and it indicated that Mexico was running through money at an incredible pace. Volcker had thought that the $700 million would last until September. Then, he thought, Mexico could work out a plan with the International Monetary Fund to obtain more funds while tightening its belt; this would also give commercial banks a more solid base on which to lend. President Jose Lopez-Portillo was not seen as a strong leader, and Silva-Herzog needed time to push the president to the IMF. A new president, Miguel de la Madrid, would take over in September, and he would be even more amenable to the IMF.

That was the plan. Now it had been frustrated by events—overspending and capital flight in Mexico. Volcker knew that something had to be done instantly. If the markets woke up Monday morning to hear that Mexico was out of money and there was no response by the U.S. or other countries, it could trigger a financial crisis that could topple the fragile world economy into a depression.

Volcker laid it on the line to Chucho. He expressed his skepticism about Lopez-Portillo's commitment to the IMF, and the finance minister assured him that the outgoing president would change his mind and become supportive when he made his own State of the Union message on September 1. The chairman told Silva-Herzog that Mexican officials must get together with the commercial banks. These banks, while easy with their lending, were now growing skittish after fears of a default by Poland and by Argentina during the Falklands War. Since a default would slam the profits of the big banks, Mexico would have to find a way to keep up interest payments while deferring principal.

Volcker passed on to the Mexican official a list of private telephone numbers of the leading American bankers. The chairman always had these numbers available to him. In the event of a fast-breaking financial crisis, he needed to know where to reach the major American financiers, whether they were at the beach, the mountains, or off in some foreign country. Silva-Herzog called the bankers over the weekend, and from that emerged a bankers' committee that negotiated with Mexico for the next several years.

Volcker figured that Mexico could get some $4 billion through a deal with the IMF in addition to a restructuring of its debt. But an emergency financing package would be needed in the meantime. He told Silva-Herzog that he would call various central banks around the world to arrange financing through the Bank of International Settlements (BIS), based in Basel, Switzerland. The chairman began to call his colleagues and, before the weekend was over, had assurances of a $1.5 billion package through the BIS, as well as a BIS meeting the next week. Of the $1.5 billion, the Fed would put up $750 million.

Volcker was perhaps the only official in the world who could arrange such a package on short notice. But he would need help. He worked closely with the head of the Bank of England, Gordon Richardson, a man he had known for a long time.

The White House was almost totally unaware of the seriousness of the situation. "Believe me, Mexico was the last thing on our mind then," a senior White House official said. "This thing came out of the blue."

It did so because Treasury Secretary Regan had not given it adequate attention. Some of Regan's staff members knew how serious the situation was, but Regan was influenced by others in his department who felt that the market could take care of the situation or that Mexico would never go bankrupt or that the U.S. government should not be a party to lending to a corrupt, inefficient regime.

But Friday the 13th woke up the administration, and the next few days, known as the "Mexican weekend," dropped like a bombshell on the administration's economic policy. Already the president was being forced to raise taxes after the huge 1981 tax cut. Now he was going to have to help bail out Mexico. It was quite a way for a conservative, free-market administration to have to come to grips with the realities of the world.

THE "MEXICAN WEEKEND"

In a furious weekend of negotiation, Mexico and the Treasury—with Volcker's assistance—worked out the emergency package. Regan assigned the job of working out the deal to his deputy, Timothy McNamar, a business-man with a bundle of ideas but without the international expertise to go with it. Before the weekend was out, the entire emergency package would total about $4 billion, with about $3 billion coming from the United States in the form of central bank loans, emergency food credits, and a purchase of Mexican oil.

It was the Mexican oil purchase that proved the most controversial. Volcker, who was at the Treasury for most of the weekend, pushed ahead the idea advanced first by Mexico and then by McNamar. Once, when a U.S. nego-tiator said that paying cash for oil would make it too expensive, Volcker snapped, "I don't give a damn what you pay for oil. If you don't do it, the whole thing is going to come crashing down, and it will be your fault." As it turned out, the U.S. got a bargain price for the Mexican oil, a 20 percent discount. Regan boasted about that later to President Reagan, who told him: "You are one hard-hearted SOB."

It was touch and go for the Mexican package for the next few months. Volcker worked closely with the Mexi-cans, the commercial banks, and the IMF, chiefly through his close friend, Jacques de Larosiere, the IMF managing director and his fishing partner. Everyone knew that the world had changed for good. It was somewhat akin to the

1971 closing of the gold window, in which Volcker had participated. From this point out, he knew, there would be constant haggling among parties and a need for the world community to work more closely together than it had ever worked before.

After that fateful weekend, Volcker used his offices and influence to get the commercial bankers and the Mexicans together. The bank advisory committee that had been formed as a result of that weekend proved to be critical. A high Citicorp executive, William Rhodes, became the co-chairman, and he worked with Volcker without the kind of tension that seemed to characterize Volcker-Wriston meetings. Since Volcker and Wriston disagreed so sharply on the debt issue and whether funds should have been lent so liberally they would not have worked well together. The first big meeting occurred at the New York Fed on August 20, with Silva-Herzog laying out the Mexican problem and seeking cooperation from commercial bankers. Although there were many questions, the Mexican finance minister left that session feeling he had support for the package.

Lopez-Portillo, though, confirmed Volcker's doubts. His State of the Union speech on September 1 was defiant. He criticized the greed of speculators working with the private banks, and he denounced the IMF, comparing its austerity prescription for Mexico with witch doctors who would want to "deprive the patient of food and subject him to compulsory rest." U.S. bankers, many of them attending the annual IMF/World Bank meeting in Toronto, became extremely apprehensive. As quoted by the late journalist Joseph Kraft, Wriston said of that IMF meeting: "We had 150-odd finance ministers, 50-odd central bankers, 1,000 journalists, 1,000 commercial bankers, a large supply of whiskey, and a reasonably small city that produced an enormous head of steam driving the engine called 'the end of the world is coming.' "

SPEAK LOUDLY AND
CARRY A BIG STICK

Enter Volcker. The day after Labor Day, September 7, would be the day to watch. There was a run on funds at the Mexican branch banks in New York. The branch banks issued checks for $70 million but did not have the funds to cover them. They turned to American banks, and two of them, Chemical and Manufacturers Hanover, came up short through the bank clearinghouse system where debts are canceled out at the end of the day. Volcker ordered $70 million deposited from the $1.5 billion BIS money.

Next, to make sure that this didn't erupt into a crisis before the package could be settled with the IMF, Volcker pressured the Mexicans. They were not to honor demands for repayments of deposits unless they were certain of a lawsuit. After that, the situation got better, although Volcker had to keep a close eye on the situation until the deal was settled.

Volcker and his friend de Larosiere stood firm against Mexico's efforts to try to keep its spending high and interest rates low and to impose exchange controls and keep wages high. Lopez-Portillo's ranting would come to naught, and he settled down. He told former Treasury undersecretary Ed Yeo that he was resigned to an IMF accord. Silva-Herzog sided with Volcker and the IMF, although the head of the Mexican central bank, Carlos Tello, sought the generous concessions on interest rates, currency controls, and wages. First Volcker, then de Larosiere, said no to Tello on October 22. Shortly afterward, Mexico caved in and agreed to the IMF's austere terms to cut its budget, raise taxes, reduce wage increases, slash subsidies, and cut its foreign borrowing from $20 billion in 1981 to $5 billion in 1983. Inflation was to be fought with austerity.

Both de Larosiere and Volcker knew that U.S. and

foreign commercial banks could not abandon Mexico. They would have to continue to lend. And de Larosiere had a big stick in the closet. On November 16 at the New York Federal Reserve Bank, he laid it out to the assembled bankers from across the world. Unless they agreed to put up an additional $5 billion, he would recommend against approval of the IMF package. Volcker, who had been clued in on this plan beforehand, followed through with a speech that took a good-guy approach. If new loans enabled a country to strengthen its economy and pay off its debt in an orderly way, the Fed would be lenient in the way it treated such loans from a regulatory standpoint, he said. In other words, they would not be criticized at all.

After much nurturing and many meetings, telephone calls, concessions, and tough stands, Volcker helped put together the Mexican rescue package of 1982. Other countries would follow, but the pattern had been set. Each nation would be considered on a case-by-case basis. Each would have to buckle under to some tough measures before any more money would be forthcoming.

But the austerity approach would not last. It put too much of a stranglehold on the developing world, giving it little room to grow. Slowly but surely, the debt strategy of the U.S. began to evolve. When Regan left the Treasury, James A. Baker III came over from the White House, where he was chief of staff, and devised a new plan that would give the Third World a little more room to grow. In return for less bone-crushing conditions imposed by the IMF and more money, debtor countries would have to reform their economies away from the counterproductive state-run systems. Baker outlined this plan at the annual IMF meeting in Seoul, Korea, in 1985, but it was Volcker who had played a large role in its conception. The chairman, though, did not want to take credit for the ideas publicly.

DEBT IS DEBT

Volcker and Baker agreed on one thing: debt is debt. They

did not favor plans, such as that proposed by Senator Bill Bradley (D., New Jersey), that the debt should be forgiven in any kind of complex scheme. Debt forgiveness only made lenders skittish in the future, they said. Once when the Fed's vice chairman of the time, Preston B. Martin, suggested in a speech that some form of debt forgiveness might have to be part of the picture, Volcker became extremely angry. In Tokyo at the time, he telephoned his press officer, Joseph R. Coyne, and fired off a statement rebuking the vice chairman for making such a suggestion. That indiscretion may have cost Martin any hopes he had of succeeding Volcker as chairman. Martin made an enemy that day in Treasury Secretary Baker, who happened to be seated next to Volcker in a hotel room when he telephoned his rebuke to Coyne.

Many critics did not like the Baker/Volcker approach. To them, it only piled debt on top of debt, rewarded the corruption and undelivered promises of the debtor nations, and amounted to throwing good money after bad. Many bankers did not appreciate what they considered to be Volcker's strong-arm tactics in getting them to ante up more money. "I just wish he weren't so hung up on throwing money at a problem," one of them said.

Volcker felt that, if Mexico was unable to make its payments, then other large debtors like Argentina and Brazil would follow, bringing down the entire house of cards. He became extremely anxious as oil prices continued to plummet, and he began to confer with Baker on how the U.S. government should respond. Once again Mexico would be the test of the U.S. debt strategy.

"NINJA" GOES TO MEXICO

Once again Volcker would go into his ninja role. It was June 1986, and Mexico was again in deep financial trouble. It was evident that the nation would run out of funds with the price of oil falling into the $10-a-barrel range and be unable to make its debt payments.

The huge decline in oil prices had clearly put Mexico, with its nearly $100 billion in debt payments, in a bind. Faced with growing political pressure from Mexico's left wing, the U.S. feared President Miguel de la Madrid Hurtado might be forced into defaulting on that country's loans to Western banks.

So it was in the spring of 1986 that Volcker decided to go to Mexico, with the blessing of the Reagan administration, Baker in particular, and the Mexican government. The Mexicans trusted Volcker; he had played straight with them before in 1982. Volcker did not carry the political baggage that an official from the White House would. Reagan's National Security Council held a grudge against de la Madrid for his strong stand on the Contra aid question, and the Mexican president knew it. The administration needed someone with credibility to go to Mexico, and Volcker was it.

There was intense debate inside the Baker Treasury on how to deal with Mexico. Some of Baker's advisors believed that the best strategy would be to force de la Madrid to the brink of default, so that the U.S. could wring greater concessions out of him. They did not share fears that the political situation in Mexico was deteriorating so fast that it could soon spin out of control and that de la Madrid's choices were highly limited. But Volcker did not want to wait and neither did Baker. "The situation was slipping away from us," said one of Volcker's advisors. "We were losing control."

Volcker discussed his trip with Baker and learned that the U.S. was willing to put its support behind a huge new loan package that would include for the first time some important concessions to Mexico. The U.S. would be willing to let Mexico reduce its payments if the price of oil remained low and if its economy did not grow as fast as hoped. The IMF also was coming around to this point of view. Mexico, of course, would have to launch a program to reform its state-owned industries and free up its trade. For this, the U.S., the IMF, World Bank, and commercial banks would all participate in a huge new loan package that would ultimately total $12 billion.

With the same kind of stealth he had used in previous trips, Volcker flew with an advisor to Houston on Sunday, June 8. There a plane owned by the Mexican central bank, with Silva-Herzog on it, met him. The transfer worked without a hitch. "Ninja" was out of the country without being spotted and soon was in Mexico City, ready to deal with the Mexicans. There, they stayed overnight in the home of the minister of tourism.

The next morning, over breakfast with de la Madrid in the presidential palace, Volcker outlined the offer of assistance to the Mexican president. Although the Reagan administration did not regard him as a strong leader, de la Madrid was sophisticated in economic matters and understood well that his country was at a crossroads. Volcker spoke calmly but forcefully about the consequences of a default and urged the president to accept the U.S. offer. "He was tremendously effective," noted the U.S. advisor.

It became clear to Volcker that de la Madrid had not been informed of the degree of assistance the U.S. was willing to offer, especially the oil and growth concessions. Had Silva-Herzog been holding out for some complex political reason that would enable him to get credit for the deal on terms favorable to Mexico? Silva-Herzog had political ambitions of his own and had been saying publicly that Mexico might default. In many respects, he overshadowed the Mexican president. At any rate, de la Madrid expressed delight at the U.S. offer and indicated that Mexico would be willing to hold up its part of the bargain.

Volcker's breakfast meeting with de la Madrid turned the situation around in Mexico, according to his closest advisors. Treasury officials might try to argue in retrospect that Volcker gave away the store, one Fed aide said, but all this had been cleared with Baker in advance. He added that the political situation in Mexico made a default "quite possible" and that Volcker's trip had instilled confidence in both sides in a highly dangerous situation. Silva-Herzog was ousted by de la Madrid within ten days after Volcker's visit, and the Fed chairman returned to Washington confident that Mexico could weather the crisis if it made the painful internal adjustments necessary.

Even then, it would take months for the Mexicans to work out the details of the loan package with the International Monetary Fund and the commercial banks, and at times it appeared the deal still might fall through. The subsequent negotiations among commercial banks to work out the details of the package were some of the most difficult and painstaking in the history of the Third World debt problem. Volcker interposed himself in these talks, wheedling and cajoling to get both sides to settle. In this connection, he worked closely with de Larosiere.

SPLITTING THE DIFFERENCE

Volcker called the bank advisory committee to Washington for a meeting at the IMF headquarters with de Larosiere and Barber Conable, president of the World Bank. It was a long, difficult negotiation, but it was apparent that the two sides were growing extremely close. They were separated by only an eighth of a percentage point. Volcker finally told them, late into the evening, that they were so close together that "by God, they ought to split the difference." That's the way it turned out.

"The banks thought that Volcker had pushed them too hard," Conable said later. "I didn't have any way of judging that, and I thought he was constructive. Paul is a man who commands a great deal of confidence from people who are dealing with him. My impression of his participation in that negotiation was that, while Jacques had the lead on it, Paul was kind of a balance wheel. His assessment of what would go and what wouldn't go was very important to the other participants." The compromise finally came about, Conable said, largely as the result of "the impasse over a ridiculous period of time over an eighth of a percentage point and the growing sense of the ridiculousness of the whole monetary system being put at risk over that narrow a spread. I think there was a general acknowledgment on the part of both the banks and the Mexicans that, after a while, neither side was going to blink, and therefore the way to go was to split the difference."

The $6 billion in bank participation (actually more when contingency proposals were included) was more than Volcker thought was possible at the beginning of the negotiations. He was skeptical that the banks would ever agree to that much money. In one sense, he was right. It would take much convincing. The agreement hinged on the negotiating committee's lining up new loans from scores of regional banks in the United States that had participated in the 1982 Mexican bailout. But these banks were not enthusiastic about the new plan, fearing that any new loans would not be paid back in full or ultimately would be written down in value, affecting their profits. The job of persuading banks to participate was not easy for the chairman of the Fed; in his view, he could only plead, not threaten, and he often did this by meeting with groups of bankers, laying out the problem, and urging greater participation.

Volcker could be tough in this regard, one highly placed source said. Continental Illinois Bank of Chicago, which in effect had been nationalized in 1984 at Volcker's and the Reagan administration's urging, had agreed to put up $60 million in new money to Mexico. Volcker told the bank bluntly that that was not enough, that Continental's participation should be $90 million. "John Swearingen [then Continental chairman] drew a line in the sand and said, 'absolutely not; we aren't going to give in more,' but eventually he caved in to Volcker's pressure and agreed to put up another $15 million for a total of $75 million," the source added.

THE "MENU" APPROACH: A MODEL?

It was well into 1987 before the Mexican package was finally wrapped up. Although Volcker, along with Baker, the IMF, and World Bank, had nursed it along carefully, it had been a wearying experience. The constant fighting over loan terms and government policies and pressuring bankers to do things they clearly did not want to do took their toll. Despite the ultimate victory, Volcker felt a sense of frustration with the process. He sensed that others were wearying of the process, too, but he saw no other alternative. Some bankers, in fact, felt that the Volcker pressure may have delayed ultimate implementation of the deal and doomed the "big package" approach to the Third World debt problem.

Volcker naturally doesn't agree that his role was counterproductive; just the opposite. But he does agree that new approaches are needed to replace the "big package" approach in which the large banks with the biggest exposure in the Third World teamed with Volcker to pressure banks with less exposure to put up funds. The regional banks with less exposure will have to be lured into participation with the promise of better terms or equity participation. They will not necessarily have the same deal as the larger banks. The Mexican bailout brought this "menu" approach to bank financing to the fore, and it could well be the model for future financings, said a U.S. financial official. Volcker himself concedes the Mexican package papered over many differences in the banking community that would have to be resolved in future such deals.

Although many members of Congress proposed debt-relief packages, Volcker constantly argued against this "solution." While some future administration might find this approach as a way out of the crisis, he said it has enormous practical problems. "How do you define that? How much, which countries, how do you control the process? It's kind of a bureaucratization of the whole international financial scene and somebody dictating in the political process who gets how much debt relief." With debtor nations already highly sensitive over the differing interest rates each must pay to the commercial banks, Volcker said it would be an extremely difficult political process to adopt a plan calling for forgiving loans or softening interest-rate terms. Any country that felt that it was not getting as good a debt-relief program as the next would argue for equal terms. The political pressure for relief would be enormous, and what commercial bank would want to lend under these circumstances?

DID VOLCKER CAUSE THE THIRD WORLD DEBT CRISIS?

The Third World debt crisis had its roots in the energy crisis of the 1970s. When OPEC quadrupled its oil prices in 1973, and oil-rich kingdoms such as Saudi Arabia and Kuwait began to accumulate enormous money surpluses, poor countries without any oil found their energy bills rising dramatically. Rather than lend their newly gained riches to the Third World directly, OPEC countries suddenly awash in a sea of cash found it easier to park their funds in Western commercial banks. Volcker, then undersecretary of the Treasury for monetary affairs, calmed fears that the OPEC countries would hold on to their cash, putting the West into a depression. "They aren't going to bury it in the sand," he said. The newly rich oil producers were perfectly happy to turn the role of recycling these "petrodollars" to the Third World over to the commercial banks, which saw an opportunity to profit as intermediaries.

But it was not until the second OPEC oil price increase of 1979 that the debt problem really became serious. It roughly coincided with Volcker's appointment to the Fed, giving rise to an oft-asked question: Was Volcker himself responsible for the Third World debt crisis?

"The Fed's tight money caused the debt problem,"
Wriston said. "World exports doubled in the decade before
that. The GNP of many developing countries doubled in
ten years. Nothing like that has ever happened in the
history of the world. When the U.S. was thrown into a
recession, so was the rest of the world. That started the
protectionist danger that exists today: Let's block out
Brazil's exports, so on and so forth. So it is circular. I am
not saying that Volcker and the Fed were responsible for
the debt crisis. As a friend of mine in the labor movement
taught me in the New York City financial crisis, every
solution carries with it the seeds of the next problem. It's
not a one-on-one relationship. But there is no question that
the severity of the economic difficulties was a contributing
factor. So were the oil prices, and so was the war in the
Falkland Islands."

A second critic, economist Edward Bernstein of the
Brookings Institution, said that commercial banks were
raking in so much money that they didn't care about the
danger of a debt crisis. The real surge in lending occurred
after the 1979 oil-price increase, he noted. "Where was the
IMF? Where was the Federal Reserve Board? These are
the people who were supposed to be watching. It almost
sounds as if we had inadequate supervision of what the
banks were doing."

A third critic, supply-side economist Paul Craig Roberts, said in congressional testimony in 1986 that "Volcker
unexpectedly plunged the world into recession and collapsed the prices of commodities that were the basis for
debt service and loan repayment by Third World countries.
Overnight, the great achievement, as it was called, of
petrodollar recycling through financial intermediaries such
as U.S. banks was turned into a very big problem. The
Federal Reserve—indeed, the entire U.S. government—
was slow to recognize the massive problem that had been
created by the Federal Reserve's serious departure from
administration policy."

Roberts went on to say that it was not until August of

1982, when Volcker learned of the potential of a Mexican default, "that he realized that he had collapsed the asset values underlying the world debt structure, thus creating a serious financial crisis."

Actually, Volcker saw the problem coming long before that. The 1982 Mexican announcement had been anticipated; indeed, the Fed had been lending to Mexico via currency swaps for months. Long before that, when the lending began to explode after the 1979 oil price increase, he had tried to persuade banks to curtail lending.

Nancy Teeters, who served on the board at the time, disclosed that Volcker and the Fed were rebuffed shortly after the 1979 oil price increase when they tried to talk the banks into curbing their lending to developing countries. Vice chairman Fred Schultz also recalls Volcker efforts to scale back the lending, adding that they met with little success. He said he recalls a meeting about this time of the Fed's own Federal Advisory Council, of which Wriston was a member, when the subject of Third World loans came up. "Wriston said, 'These are the best loans I've got. My loss ratio on international loans is the lowest category of any type of loan,' " Schultz said. "And then I remember Wriston making that claim he made over and over again: 'Sovereign nations don't go broke.' "

Volcker, though, did not raise the public alarm about the Third World debt crisis until it had already become apparent. This indicated that, although he was worried about the surge in lending in a general way, he did not fully foresee the extent of the debt crisis that was to develop when the recession took hold. The level of interest rates that resulted from the Fed's tight-money policies surprised him, and the depth of the recession was clearly not anticipated. But Volcker was not alone in failing to have a clairvoyant view of the future. No one else saw well enough ahead to predict how serious the debt crisis would become.

Teeters said that, if the Fed had not held on to tight money for so long, the recession would not have been so deep, and perhaps the debt crisis might have been postponed. "But I believe the Latin American debt crisis would have happened anyway. The developing countries were already overextended. The recession just made it happen sooner," she said.

The 1979 oil price increase created huge demands for dollars by the developing nations, and it would have been difficult for Volcker to stem the tide if he had gone public and taken on the nation's largest banks directly. As Thibaut de Saint Phalle notes in a recent book on the Federal Reserve, the second oil price increase was much worse because it began from a high base, taking the price from $13 a barrel to $40 a barrel at its peak. "When you consider the demands of developing countries that had been rapidly industrializing in the intervening years, it is easy to understand the effect of this massive new price increase," he noted.

As a result of Volcker's policies, interest rates rose, boosting the Third World's borrowing costs. The subsequent recession made the U.S. less hungry for the goods of the developing countries, hurting their economies. When U.S. commercial banks saw the collapse in developing-country exports on which their loans were based, they scaled back their lending, making the problem worse. At the same time, a fast-developing oil glut reduced the revenues of oil producers, so they had less money to recycle, and commercial bank lending to debt-ridden countries declined rapidly.

When all this became clear in 1982, the debt problem was a full-blown crisis. A staff study for Congress's Joint Economic Committee noted that, in 1982, U.S. commercial banks had a total loan exposure of $83.9 billion in Latin America, more than one-quarter of its total debt. The U.S. commercial banking system's total exposure in Latin America at the end of 1982 equaled 119 percent of the total capital for all major banks while the Latin American exposure of nine money center banks equaled 176 percent of their combined capital.

The study noted: "On average, all nine money center banks would have failed if the Latin American debtors announced they could repay only 40 percent of their outstanding debt. Even if they said they would repay as much as 80 percent of the outstanding debt, the nine money center banks stood to lose more than 35 percent of their combined capital. Their ability to continue functioning and extending credit to U.S. borrowers would be seriously impaired. Clearly, U.S. officials were correct in perceiving that the debt crisis was a serious threat to the U.S. banking system—and to the U.S. economy."

The same study noted that, in spite of these difficulties, U.S. commercial banks found the Third World market an incredibly profitable enterprise. The debt problem enabled them to increase their spreads—the difference between what they pay for deposits and what they charge for loans. In 1980, these spreads averaged 86 basis points (100 points equals 1 percent interest). By 1983, some banks tripled their spreads, and in 1986 they averaged 125 basis points. As a result of the higher margins, money-center banks were able to increase their profits dramatically, the study noted.

Volcker became part and parcel of this, but not because he was out to help bank profitability at the expense of developing countries. Once the crisis became reality, the only practical choice of policymakers was to encourage banks to continue lending in the Third World, something they were not that eager to do considering the risk. The higher the risk, the higher the interest rate.

The Third World debt crisis occupied much of Volcker's time and worry after 1982. Behind the scenes, he played a big role in putting together lending packages, awakening the public's mind to the crisis, pressuring banks to put up more of their money, and developing an overall strategy for dealing with the crisis. His fear for the future is that the developed countries will become fatigued in dealing with the problem or that world economic growth will slow down to the point that the debtor nations will lose some of their international markets, thus deepening the crisis.

Volcker believes the debt problem is manageable. Commercial banks are gradually reducing these troubled loans from their portfolios, he noted, but it will still take time, and good luck, before the risk is tamed. Some of his advisors believe that it will require another decade before the risk to the international financial system has diminished.

Whether he "caused" it or not, the debt crisis gave Volcker's negotiating and crisis-management abilities severe tests. His handling of the Mexican crisis in 1982, when the White House thought its own Treasury Department was asleep at the switch, improved his stature with Reagan administration politicians who had distrusted him. It dramatically improved his chances for reappointment in 1983.

The debt crisis took a new and troublesome turn in 1987. Two events made it appear that the Baker/Volcker strategy would have to be revised. First, Brazil, one of the largest debtors, declared a moratorium on its interest payments. Second, Citicorp, led by John S. Reed, Wriston's successor, announced that it was in effect writing down the value of some $3 billion in Third World loans. It did so by putting funds in reserve to cover potential losses from these loans, a practice known as provisioning.

Although Brazil ultimately softened its stance and also announced a new economic policy to combat roaring inflation, the decision by such a big debtor to confront U.S. banks left many with fears that eventually the Baker/ Volcker strategy could not work because of repeated instances of this type. Perhaps some form of debt forgiveness would have to be part of the solution, no matter how much both men hated it.

Although Baker and Volcker both praised Citicorp's action, privately they both disagreed sharply with Reed. It clearly was an aggressive move by the bank; it would put

Citicorp in a better bargaining position to deal with debtors. If the bank had already assumed some of the loans were no good, a debtor nation asking for relief would not be in a strong position.

Other money-center U.S. banks followed Citicorp's actions; they had little choice. It signalled to the debtor nations that it was going to get tougher to obtain additional money from commercial banks. Since the Baker/ Volcker plan relied so heavily on commercial bank participation (over $20 billion worth), its viability was in question.

12
FOUR MORE YEARS
AND THE
DOLLAR SEESAW

As the inflation that had pounded the U.S. economy for so many years receded in the sunset after 1982, Paul Volcker became a folk hero in the financial markets of the United States and in the world. At last, they said, a Federal Reserve chairman had shown some guts and tenacity against the powerful forces of inflation.

With an ego as majestic as his height, Volcker carried this status nicely in his public appearances. Whenever he testified on Capitol Hill, a large press corps showed up to take down every word, and after he was finished they followed him in the corridors, peppering him with questions. "Volcker's Army," some called them. Unless he had something specific he wanted to get across to the markets that day, Volcker usually brushed off the press, poking gentle fun at the questions or ignoring them. He was always in control.

Volcker recognized the need for the Federal Reserve chairman to have power; it enhanced the status of the institution he loved. Deep down, he loved the attention and respect as well; his wife once said jokingly that he would like to be Fed chairman for life. But as always with this reserved man, there was a reluctance to grab on to power with the complete zest that a professed politician would. Asked if he considered himself the second most powerful man in Washington, he responded with a distinct laugh known to his friends as his "nervous laugh." No, he said, he didn't, and he wished the phrase would go away. Furthermore, he said, the phrase made him and the Fed something of a sitting duck politically, and he wished the press would stop using it.

After Volcker had relaxed and let money grow beyond his monetary targets, the economy in 1983 began recovering from the recession, but there was no question that markets were still jittery. The Reagan White House began focusing on an important question: Should Volcker be appointed to a second term (on August 6, 1983, his four-year term as chairman would expire)? Volcker's Fed term was for fourteen years, but he would never have gone back to being a board member after having been chairman. First, Volcker had to debate the question with himself and his own family. Did he want the job again? His wife, Barbara, did not like the separation and would have preferred that he not seek a second term, but she made it clear that she did not want to be the heavy and deny him the opportunity.

His son, Jimmy, had made enormous progress in recovering from his previous operations and his lack of confidence. He became interested in banking and took courses at New York University. His teacher in some classes was, ironically enough, Volcker's old friend, Robert Kavesh. Jimmy landed a job at National Westminster Bank in New York and began working on plans for advancement. His handicap was entirely physical; he got around with braces. His parents had stressed to him that he must learn to cope in the world himself despite his handicap— and that he had done.

Volcker had his enemies within the administration.

Initially, Treasury Secretary Donald Regan opposed his reappointment. Presidential advisor Edwin Meese III wanted the Fed vice chairman and a fellow Californian, Preston B. Martin, to get the job. Martin Anderson, Reagan's top domestic advisor until he resigned to go back to California, said Volcker had done a fine job but recommended that the president choose his own man as chairman of the Fed. The White House began focusing on the reappointment question after the economic summit conference in Williamsburg, Virginia. The names suggested by top aides included Volcker; Martin; economist Alan Greenspan; Paul W. McCracken, who was chairman of President Nixon's Council of Economic Advisers; Citicorp chairman Walter Wriston; and two monetarists, Milton Friedman and Beryl Sprinkel, undersecretary of the Treasury for monetary affairs.

Volcker met with Reagan on June 6 and discussed reappointment. He made clear to the president that, if he was reappointed, he would not want to commit himself to a full four years. In spite of later reports, there was no deal for him to resign after a year or so, giving Reagan the opportunity to appoint his own man. Some people in the White House had the distinct impression that Volcker would step down after a couple of years, partly based on family considerations. The Fed chief had, after all, made financial sacrifices in his post and was worried that he wasn't being fair to his family. At his session with Reagan, though, Volcker spent much of the time discussing the danger of the Third World debt crisis. Since he had excelled in this area, his remarks could not have been a better recommendation for his reappointment.

Volcker helped his own cause through his long associations in Washington. He had developed his own private network of friends and associates who could talk up his name in the power corridors. Some of this fed back to the White House. The Senate majority leader, Howard Baker, who had criticized Volcker privately on occasion, had great respect for Volcker and urged his reappointment. So did the president's closest associate in Congress, Senator Paul Laxalt (R., Nevada).

THE MARKETS REAPPOINT VOLCKER

More than anything else, though, there were the markets. With budget deficits in the neighborhood of $200 billion, the Reagan administration had lost credibility in the financial markets; Volcker had earned their respect. This was buttressed by a poll of financial market executives showing that they overwhelmingly favored Volcker's reappointment.

The choice narrowed to Volcker and Greenspan. Greenspan stayed in the running because he was a Reagan economic advisor from the beginning of the 1980 campaign. He had solid Republican credentials and was prominent enough to be known by the markets. For those supporting Volcker, he was a good, middle-of-the-road fallback.

Oddly enough, Greenspan didn't win any friends among the president's economic advisors. Regan saw him as a greater threat than Volcker. Greenspan had been an independent force as chairman of President Ford's Council of Economic Advisers. At least Volcker was a known entity and, in spite of some rocky moments, had worked with Treasury. Supply-side gurus like Jude Wanniski didn't like Greenspan because they feared he would be an even tighter money man than Volcker. They preferred Volcker's flexibility, they said, over what they perceived would be Greenspan's staunch monetarism.

Meese stuck with his candidate, Martin, almost to the end. Budget Director Stockman and Martin Feldstein, chairman of the Council of Economic Advisers, urged Volcker's reappointment. White House chief of staff James A. Baker III, a pragmatist like Volcker, spoke for reappointment, turning the tide. In the end, though, the perception flowed from the White House that it was the markets, not the president, who reappointed Volcker. With the economic times still perilous and the presidential election coming up in 1984, the president decided against upsetting the markets. As one administration official put it at the time: "We didn't reappoint Volcker. The markets reappointed Volcker." Herbert Stein, an unofficial Reagan advisor who had served as President Nixon's chief economic advisor, said if Volcker had not been reappointed it would "send a signal that the political authorities don't appreciate what Mr. Volcker has done."

Back in Volcker's New York apartment, when the news came over the radio, Barbara Volcker sat down at the kitchen table and cried.

Volcker didn't want to give up the Fed just yet. Reappointment was more than a matter of personal pride. He felt his work hadn't been finished. Inflation was down and, in fact, would fall under 4 percent in 1983, but it was nothing special to see it collapse under the weight of such a severe recession. Would it stay down when the recovery got rolling? The banking system he supervised was sill vulnerable, and the Third World debt crisis had the potential of causing an economic crash. No, it was not yet time to depart. He wanted to see it through. "We have to recognize that stabilizing prices at a time of the most severe recession in 40 years is in no sense 'victory,'" he said at the time. "The only real achievement will be found in a noninflationary economic expansion. . . . We were in a no-win situation in the 1970s. We may be in a win situation in the 1980s."

THE NEW OPPOSITION: REAGAN APPOINTEES

The White House clearly had its own ideas about control of the central bank, however. Since the Fed played such a key role in the Reagan era, and since so many political operatives saw it as one of Washington's key power centers, the administration paid more attention to the political importance of Fed appointments than did previous administrations. The White House ignored Volcker's recommendations of board members, while the Nixon and Ford administrations had for the most part acquiesced to Arthur F. Burns's recommendations. Burns himself thought the administration was treating Volcker shamefully and so told the White House, but it did not make any difference.

As a matter of practice, Volcker thought that the chairman ought to have an informal power of veto over appointments to the board of governors. Indeed, he protested to the White House some candidates whose names had been mentioned in speculation and successfully blocked some of them; they might never have been appointed anyway, but Volcker at least registered his feeling.

He wasn't excited about Preston Martin's appointment as vice chairman, but didn't object after the man Martin was to replace, Fred Schultz, told Volcker that Martin had a good record in the financial arena and should be given a chance. Martin, a former chairman of the Federal Home Loan Bank Board, had close connections in the Reagan White House, especially with Edwin Meese, but he was a Fed outsider. Almost from the beginning, Volcker and Martin didn't get on. William O'Connell, president of the U.S. League of Savings Institutions, noticed while sitting in on a meeting with Volcker and Martin that "the tension between them was palpable."

From Volcker's perspective, Martin had his own agenda that included angling to be chairman one day. Martin hired his own public relations person and became a visible vice chairman. From Martin's perspective, Volcker had ruled the Fed with an iron hand and had kept money too tight for too long. When he came onto the board, he noted that it was made up primarily of former staff members, an institution that was highly insular and kept perpetuating itself through a cozy method of appointment. As a man who had just come from private industry, he had seen firsthand the pain and suffering in American industry caused by Volcker's tight-money policies. The danger of inflation returning any time soon, he thought, was extremely slight.

Of similar persuasion was Martha Seger, a Michigan banking regulator named to succeed Nancy Teeters on the board. The Seger nomination was notable in one sense. When she was sworn in at the White House in the Rose Garden, a sensitive microphone of a television reporter caught Volcker complaining about all the lobbyists that had been invited to the ceremony. The Seger-Volcker relationship went downhill after that, but Seger, because of her limited background in monetary policy, never became the threat that Martin did. She complained about Volcker's dominating influence and about his smelly cigars.

1984: THE GOLDEN YEAR

Volcker's policies really began to pay off in 1983 and especially in 1984, when inflation remained low and economic growth began to pick up. Since 1984 was a presidential election year, the emergence of high growth and low inflation was perfect from a reelection standpoint. But Volcker once again proved he was capable of taking on the White House. In the spring of 1984, with the economy booming along, the Federal Reserve decided to tighten again. There was a fear that growth could get out of control, and the money supply itself would explode. (Although the Fed by this time had deemphasized the money supply numbers, they were not viewed as unimportant. Excessive growth would be a sign that it had given up on fighting inflation.)

The White House issued a statement critical of the Fed for not being "accommodative." Supply-side guru Wanniski, who had supported Volcker's reappointment, was especially critical. Donald Regan carried on a Fed-bashing crusade so sharp that the White House finally had to call it off because it was upsetting the markets. "Where's the inflation?" said Regan time and again, echoing Walter Mondale's campaign theme, "Where's the beef?".

"The only thing overheated is overheated economists," Martin said about the fear that the economy was overheating. Many private economists said tightening was a good decision and had the effect of extending the recovery, but this viewpoint vanished the closer it got to the White House. Later in the year, the criticism of Volcker settled down, and so did economic growth. The Fed saw fit to ease again right before the election. The "crisis" over the Fed subsided. One administration official described the Fed-bashing as "standard election stuff," which Volcker well understood. The chairman had seen this come and go before and once described administration criticism of his policies as "quibbling."

From a pure monetary target standpoint, 1984 was the Fed's best year, noted economist David Jones. "In that 'golden year,' the monetary authorities hit their M1 target and did much to strengthen their anti-inflation credibility," he wrote in his authoritative book, *Fed Watching*.

Yet Volcker was cautious. He had the central banker's traditional concern with inflation, plus the memory of a painful battle to lick the 1970s inflation. "I don't think inflation is ever under control permanently," he said. "History has proved that. You keep it under control by keeping your guard up." The battle over how fast to drop interest rates continued into 1985 and 1986.

THE PALACE COUP

It was early 1986, on February 24, before all this opposition came to a head. It was the day of the so-called palace coup. Two new Reagan appointees, Manuel Johnson, an assistant secretary of the Treasury under Donald Regan, and Wayne Angell, a Kansas banker and protégé of Senate Republican Leader Bob Dole, had just taken their seats on the board. Martin at the time had been pressing for a cut in the Fed's discount rate, but Volcker had been resisting, believing that it should be coordinated with cuts in West Germany and Japan. Martin had been pressing his case for several months, to no avail.

Angell and Johnson were on Martin's side from the outset, and so was Seger. Angell said he and Johnson had talked privately about confronting Volcker on the discount-rate change and agreed that they should try. Angell said he entertained the possibility that Volcker might resign if he lost, but came to the conclusion that Volcker wanted to remain chairman above all else, so he pressed ahead.

Volcker was surprised when the discount-rate cut was pushed by Reagan appointees that morning, although technically it could be taken up since there was a recommendation for a reduction from one of its regional banks. The Fed usually acts on discount-rate changes on the basis of recommendations from one or more of the twelve regional banks. Often it turns down or delays action on these requests, which are frequently on the table. In his view, discount-rate changes occur after considerable internal discussion of several days or more or in an emergency situation, when there is little disagreement. For one to occur so abruptly, especially with the avid support of two brand-new members, was unprecedented, he thought. Volcker blamed Martin, since Martin could have stopped it if he had wanted. He was the vice chairman and the leader of the opposition. When the board voted four to three to cut the discount rates, Volcker felt that he had been blindsided. To him, it made no sense at all to barge out before the public and change the discount rate while the government was trying to persuade other countries to cut their rates. In addition, forcing a vote like that was totally outside Fed tradition and culture from Volcker's standpoint. He truly had not expected it.

A staff member who was there said the chairman should not have been surprised considering that a discount-rate change was on the table that morning. Arthur F. Burns was also surprised at the way it happened, indicating that Volcker should never have permitted things to go that far. The chairman had enough power to put off a vote, he felt. But Burns had never encountered a board as independent of the chairman's influence as the one over which Volcker presided, a totally new situation. Volcker wasn't surprised that the issue was brought up, but he thought it wouldn't be forced to a vote that day. A few days earlier, he had testified on Capitol Hill and didn't hint at any discount-rate change then. Since the meeting came so soon after this testimony, he didn't expect a showdown.

Volcker would have resigned as soon as the vote became public, as it would at the end of the day, had the situation not mysteriously turned around. The Fed chief had lunch with Treasury Secretary James Baker and Mexican Finance Minister Jesus Silva-Herzog that day, and Baker became aware of the challenge to Volcker. There are indications that Baker may have pulled some political strings to smooth over the situation, although Volcker wasn't aware of any. In the afternoon, there was a new development. Just how it happened isn't clear, but Angell went to Volcker's office and agreed to a compromise that would permit Volcker to arrange a coordinated discount-rate cut with West Germany and Japan. Angell said he was called to Volcker's office and did not initiate a meeting. Volcker's version is that Angell and Martin had passed the word they wanted to see him.

At any rate, the meeting gave Volcker the opportunity to discuss his position further and Angell the chance to give the chairman an out. It was Angell's impression that Volcker made it clear at this session that his chairmanship was at stake and put the issue of whether there should be a resignation on Angell's shoulders. Angell remembers Volcker words to this effect: "Do you want me to remain chairman?" Volcker doesn't remember it that way; he recalls that it was Angell who came in wanting to work something out and his future wasn't discussed.

Volcker and Angell met alone at first, and then Martin joined the discussion. By the time Martin got there, however, the compromise had been formulated. After it was over, the palace coup had ended; Volcker's opponents had failed to oust the king. The press release in preparation for the discount rate change was thrown away.

Martin resigned shortly thereafter and returned to the private sector. While Martin denied that he was angling for the chairmanship as Volcker suspected, a White House aide said differently—that Martin had wanted some assurance of being appointed chairman when Volcker's term expired in August 1987.

The failed palace coup did clear the air at the Fed. The Reagan appointees became much more cautious, and Volcker himself became a collegial leader. But this was clearly a new situation. No longer could Volcker dominate as he once had. Although the chairman controlled the agenda of the board meetings, a considerable power, he was forced into greater accommodation. At the same time, some of the Reagan appointees did not turn out to be as ideological as the White House thought they might. Johnson, a supply-side economist who had criticized Volcker from his Treasury post, became more of a Fed insider and did not challenge Volcker as directly as some of his old friends wanted. Volcker learned to trust Johnson, a soft-spoken economist with a friendly nature. Ironically, Johnson had said in an interview about a year before he was appointed that he thought Volcker and the Fed "were hung up on the problems of the past decade," referring to the energy and food shortages that raised prices. "All those things are past now."

THE DOLLAR SOARS

By 1985, the Fed's old restrictive policy was a shadow of its former self. With the U.S. economy slowing down and inflation in check, Volcker and the Fed virtually ignored the money supply. It was clear by now that the relationship between money growth and gross national product had broken down and no longer provided a reliable guide for internal operations. Further, Volcker wanted to ease. The exchange rate of the dollar had risen to record-high levels, pushing up the U.S. trade deficit and bringing in billions of dollars of borrowed capital from Japan and Europe. The U.S. became a net debtor nation, owing more overseas than foreign countries owned to American creditors.

The dollar began getting stronger directly as a result of Volcker's tight-money policies and the big budget deficits of the Reagan administration. Volcker never suspected the dollar would rise as high as it would. Early in the Reagan administration, he pleaded with the Treasury Department to let the Federal Reserve intervene in the currency markets to stem the speculation in the dollar and keep it from rising too high. He thought the administration made a big mistake when Treasury Undersecretary Beryl Sprinkel went to Capitol Hill early in the term and declared that, henceforth, except in times of extreme crisis, the U.S. would not intervene formally in the markets.

Volcker used words like *catastrophe* and *disaster* to describe this free-wheeling, free-market approach. Fed official Steve Axilrod said he called the Treasury frequently to try to get a change in policy, but he was always rebuffed. Administration officials had a graphic little saying to justify their no-intervention, free-market stance. With more than $100 billion being traded in currency markets daily, they said, central banks would soon go broke trying to go against the tide. "It would be like pissing in the ocean," said a member of President Reagan's Council of Economic Advisers.

Thanks to the strong dollar, the trade deficit soared, cutting back economic growth in the U.S. and making Americans import junkies. At the same time, U.S. exports declined sharply, and many American firms that had opened up overseas markets in the 1970s suddenly found themselves priced out of the market by their own currency.

"They say that one of the measurements of a good central banker is to have a strong currency, but I guess we overdid it a bit," Volcker said once in an offhand remark about what had developed.

The amount of foreign capital pouring into the U.S. was staggering—over $100 billion a year. It was helping to finance the budget deficit and to keep the economy rising even at a time when the Fed was trying to keep money tight. The capital came in because Japanese and European pension funds and insurance firms saw U.S. bonds as highly attractive investments with interest rates so high. But this money would have to be paid back with interest over time, and that interest bill would get very large. Paying this bill would slowly cut into the standard of living of Americans.

Volcker began sounding the alarm about Americans' reliance on foreign capital long before anyone else, and he put the blame on the big budget deficits, not the Federal Reserve's policies, although both clearly shared in the responsibility. At least Volcker could say he was walking the high road in trying to control inflation. Neither Congress nor the White House could be proud of its record in failing to reduce the size of the budget deficit.

VOLCKER AND BAKER: MANAGING THE DOLLAR'S DECLINE

After Reagan was reelected, Volcker's effort to obtain a more realistic exchange rate for the dollar dramatically improved when Treasury Secretary Regan decided to switch jobs with White House Chief of Staff James A. Baker III. It was a good move for Volcker because Baker shared his pragmatic view and his belief that the dollar was overvalued. Both men worked quietly together in the international area. As 1985 wore on, and it became clear that a new initiative was needed to cut the dollar's value, Baker and Volcker conferred privately with their counterparts from the key industrial countries on a plan to reduce the dollar's value. It culminated in a September 22, 1985, meeting of finance ministers and central bankers from the top seven industrial countries at the Plaza Hotel in New York. They agreed that the dollar's value was too high and should be reduced.

The Plaza agreement served its purpose of giving the dollar a strong downward shove at just the time it had already begun to fall. Over the next year and a half, it would drop by nearly 50 percent against the major world currencies. At times, the drop was so fast that it deeply concerned Volcker. He was worried about a free-fall of the dollar, one that would destroy confidence in the currency and bring back inflation. It was the kind of scenario that would force him as Fed chairman to increase interest rates dramatically to defend the dollar, risking a worldwide recession in the process.

Volcker and Baker used teamwork in managing the decline of the dollar, playing a good-guy, bad-guy routine. Baker would use rhetoric or innuendo to suggest the dollar should fall further, and it would. Then Volcker would make a public statement to the effect that the dollar was dropping too fast or had fallen far enough, and it would stabilize.

These wild swings in the dollar sobered the Fed chairman and Baker. Borrowing from an international monetary reform plan that Volcker had devised in 1972, Baker tried to bring some stability to the situation. He proposed a plan calling for the major industrial nations to coordinate their economic policies by abiding by a common set of objective economic indicators. Volcker liked the Baker plan of trying to move the U.S., Japan, and Europe back toward some semblance of fixed exchanged rates. The idea behind this proposal was to force Japan and West Germany to recognize that they must expand their economies and stop relying on exporting so much to the United States. Volcker, like Baker, wanted a "home-grown" economic expansion in Japan and Europe. With Baker handling the negotiations, President Reagan and the heads of state of the six other major industrial democracies adopted this plan at the annual economic summit in Tokyo in 1986. But the plan lacked the political teeth to force West Germany and Japan to accelerate their economies. It was watered down to a process of consultation and coordination and formally approved at the Venice economic summit in 1987.

The dollar kept sinking so rapidly that, early in 1987, Volcker put on his worry beads again. "Enough is enough," he said. He saw the signs of reemerging inflation in commodity prices, and interest rates on long-term bonds began to rise, another big inflation indicator. All those gains he had made against inflation, he feared, could go out the window if this game of competitive devaluation of the dollar did not stop. A lower dollar boosted import prices and also took pressure off domestic producers to keep their prices in competition with foreign producers.

Baker felt the same way and arranged a new currency deal with U.S. allies on February 22 at the Louvre in Paris after weeks of tedious negotiations. There the finance ministers of the major countries pledged to maintain their currency rates at more or less current levels. It was a desperate attempt to draw a line in the sand and prevent the kind of monetary instability that had plagued the industrial countries.

Volcker was intimately involved in this process. He spoke with Baker, and he was constantly on the telephone with his central-bank colleagues from other countries as the Fed actively intervened in the currency markets to prop up the dollar's value. Although he recognized that intervention had its limitations in trying to defend a precise dollar exchange rate, he saw it as a useful tool to keep the speculators off guard and to try to prevent the currency from overshooting its mark on the way down or on the way up.

But Volcker recognized that defending any currency rate would be difficult with the huge trade imbalances still hanging over the heads of the industrial countries. The huge U.S. trade deficit, which reached $169 billion in 1986, was an unstable force in itself, as were its mirror images, the trade surpluses in Japan and West Germany.

Volcker, more than anyone else on the American side, looked at the situation with a hard realism. Baker, a political creature trying to deal with Congress, pressed the Japanese and West Germans at some meetings to make vague, symbolic statements in favor of economic expansion. From experience, Volcker knew that symbolism never takes one very far in the international arena, although it might be good from a domestic political standpoint.

Volcker put his international experience and contacts into play again when Japanese Prime Minister Yashuiro Nakasone was scheduled to visit Washington in April of 1987. The dollar was still in a tailspin against the yen, largely because the Reagan administration had upset financial markets by imposing tariffs on Japanese electronic products. Working closely with Baker, Volcker worked out a deal in which the Japanese would cut interest rates and the United States would raise its interest rates. The deal was announced in the middle of Nakasone's visit, and it helped stabilize the dollar for a time.

But Volcker knew that it would take a sharp reduction in the trade deficit to turn the dollar situation around in a fundamental way. The huge trade imbalances would require big and difficult economic adjustments for Americans, if not for the rest of the world, he said. America would have to become a premier producer of goods and run a surplus in its balance of trade in the future, Volcker added, and this would mean many fundamental changes in the U.S. way of doing business.

13
THE BIG NANNY

One day early in 1987, Paul Volcker had a few investment managers from Wall Street into his office. It was the time of furious takeover activity and a rising, though extremely volatile, stock market.

Careful not to frown or growl for fear he might send the wrong signal, he used his trusted defense: the Volcker cross-examination. He asked them what they thought about the takeovers, the creation of debt, junk bonds, and all the speculation and volatility, and where all that was leading. To a man, they responded that they feared it would ultimately lead to big financial problems, perhaps a crisis. But how do they incorporate such an outlook into their financial planning? the chairman wanted to know. Not at all, they responded. They just don't let things like that bother them.

Such attitudes about debt do not surprise Volcker anymore, but they worry him deeply. They shape his attitude about the ultimate role of the Federal Reserve Board in American society. If no one else will defend the integrity of the dollar, he felt, the Fed must. He had hoped that the banking system in the United States would have been a conservative center of strength, but the Third World debt crisis proved that it was lured by high profits and not safety.

Walter Wriston loved to call Volcker the "big nanny," the man who wanted to intrude his fussy little regulatory arm into every new enterprise tried by creative financiers like Wriston. It was excessive worry, Wriston suggested; he felt the banking system had to shed the shackles of regulation so that it could better compete on a worldwide basis and even within the U.S. with new issuers of debt.

The issue, though, was not so much about regulation as it was about the overall safety of the financial system. Volcker saw the creation of debt as a cultural, sociological by-product of postwar inflation. As he put it: "Debt was not the leading edge; debt was the consequence of inflation." The United States had seen an inflationary trend all through the postwar period, he felt; it was extremely mild in the 1950s and 1960s, but the direction of it was clear in his mind. It burst forth with a vengeance in the 1970s, spurred by shortages of oil and food and by a surfeit of easy money.

Volcker saw the period after the Great Depression as an unusually stable period for the banking system. "The mere fact that you have gone through 40 years of stability helps create the forces that undermine that," he said. "People sit there, and a new generation says, 'What the hell are we doing this [being so conservative] for? We haven't had a banking crisis in 40 years. Why don't we lend some of this money to Argentina?' "

Looking at a longer time period, he feels the U.S. economy has been characterized by recurring crises that should not be taken lightly from a historical standpoint in spite of the financial safety nets established during the Depression.

This perspective in large measure explains Volcker's activism in a public career that spans a generation. Perhaps "national nanny" is not too bad a phrase if one is needed to define the essence of the man. The Federal Reserve has always arrogated to itself the responsibility for making sure that the financial system and people in general do not engage in boisterous, self-destructive behavior. Volcker personified this attitude as much as, if not more than, any other chairman. He is fond of quoting former chairman William McChesney Martin, who said the Fed's role was to take away the punch bowl just as the party was getting good.

Volcker has given Americans a unique continuity in economic leadership and policy-making, from John Kennedy's Treasury Department to the Federal Reserve under Ronald Reagan. He feels that this type of experience is sorely needed in a highly volatile world and that the chairman of the Federal Reserve, whoever he may be, should provide that kind of solid background to any new administration that comes to power. It is especially true in the international realm, where Volcker provided the Reagan administration with the depth and breadth of background it desperately needed.

Volcker gave to the Reagan administration, and to the American public, the cold, hard edge of economic realism. In doing so, he had a profound effect on the nation's economic policy.

Reagan came into office with the hope that he could cut taxes, boost military spending, and also bring inflation under control with tight money. Volcker showed him that there was no such thing as a painless cure for inflation.

Volcker also changed the administration's international economic policy. It began with a laissez-faire attitude about intervening in currency markets, but it had to back off when the dollar got too strong and to take Volcker's advice for a more active role. It began with an oblivious attitude about the Third World debt problem but quickly turned around when Mexico almost went bankrupt in 1982 and at Volcker's urging worked out a rescue plan.

The Reagan administration didn't like bailouts, either, but it found it had no other choice but to take Volcker's advice when Continental Illinois Bank and Trust Company moved to the brink of collapse in 1984. The administration swallowed its pride and nationalized the bank, hardly blinking an eye in the process. Forced to choose between pragmatism and economic ideology, the administration chose pragmatism. Volcker played a major role in the Continental rescue in encouraging bankers to rally around the Illinois bank and in supplying loans and expertise. He assigned his close friend, Gerald Corrigan, then the president of the Minneapolis Federal Reserve Bank, to handle the negotiations. Volcker was never comfortable with the bailout, but as Charles Partee, a Fed governor at the time, put it: "We had to do it to keep the financial system from exploding on us."

The system. To understand Volcker is to see how he strove mightily to maintain the existing systems with which he dealt, only to see them crumble with changing circumstances that were beyond his control. As a Treasury staff member, he saw the international monetary system of fixed exchange rates for currencies collapse, ushering in a new era of floating exchange rates. Try as he might, he could not put Humpty Dumpty together again. As Fed chairman, he was still trying. While he favored intervention in the marketplace to affect the value of the dollar, he did not like the Reagan administration's aggressive, competitive devaluation of the dollar. A nation with a fiat currency must handle it with care and respect and not use it as a weapon, he felt.

Charls Walker, who served with Volcker in the Treasury, said Volcker will be remembered for managing the end of the dollar/gold standard, bringing to a close an important era in U.S. and world economic history.

Volcker ran afoul of the Reagan administration's many banker friends when he tried to preserve much of the old regulatory structure over the banking system. He recognized that some accommodations had to be made for changing times and changing technology and communications, but he didn't like the mixing of banking and commerce in one business entity or aggressive moves by New York banks, especially Citicorp, to find loopholes in banking laws that would enable them to expand their base of operations and functions. In all this, he worried about the safety and soundness of the banking system. To those in the Reagan administration who would abolish much of this regulatory structure, Volcker was—as the chairman put it—"something of a fuddy-duddy."

Being a fuddy-duddy meant taking some positions that might seem inconsistent. It would mean favoring bank bailouts to keep the financial system afloat or extending more debt to Mexico as a solution for the Third World debt crisis. As a crisis manager in perilous times, he strove to keep the lid on.

Wriston faulted Volcker for lack of devotion to free markets and resisting efforts of the banks to break out of what he considered an outmoded, restrictive regulatory structure to offer new "products" that would compete with other financial institutions. Volcker, he said, does not have the same faith in free markets that he does. "On the regulatory side, I had a philosophical difference, not a personal difference," Wriston added. "I like to think he's a good friend of mine, and I have an enormous respect for his intellectual powers. I just come out a different door. He's been in the public sector all his life, except for a modest span as an economist at Chase, and I have been in the private sector all my life, so that's logical. I believe very strongly in open competition and free markets, and he believes very strongly that the Fed knows best and should control the world."

Just as Wriston resented Volcker's "big nanny" attitude, Reagan administration officials would go into a pique about Volcker's constant harping about the deficit. It was his Volcker-knows-best attitude that sparked the anger. Yet, Volcker had developed a coherent theory about the deficit's international implications. He was the first to see how it was sucking foreign capital into the U.S. like a huge vacuum cleaner.

Former West German Chancellor (and Finance Minister) Helmut Schmidt called Volcker "an outstanding helmsman of monetary policy in the Western world." In his book, *A Grand Strategy for the West*, Schmidt praised Volcker for warning that, "as the United States continues to draw heavily on the world's savings, there is a drag on internally generated expansion in other economies. He has emphasized repeatedly that the United States is in the process of moving from the world's largest creditor to the world's largest debtor, that there is the danger of a breakdown in the flow of funds on which the United States has depended to satisfy public and private capital needs, and that there are numerous examples of the serious consequences of excessive indebtness."

Schmidt said Volcker is "one of the few American economists whose published view is not restricted to the domestic consequences of continued American deficit spending. He is one of the very few who tries to make the American public understand the implications of the world economy. Most of the members of the Reagan administration seem to have a strong tendency to pass over the implications for the world economy (if indeed they recognize them) and to rely on their country's vast political power to handle external economic threats."

Schmidt wrote these words in 1985. By 1987, Volcker's warnings had been popularized to the point that many of the nation's political leaders and economists struck up the same theme in urging that the U.S. reduce its deficit.

Volcker had defined this issue and communicated it so well that it had become an article of economic faith in the country. Few people call him the "Great Economic Communicator," but he has been most assuredly that, despite the fact that he rarely goes on television or does on-the-record interviews. Congressional testimony, speeches, and background interviews with reporters are his main tools of communication.

Economist Herbert Stein maintained that Fed chairmen love to rail on about budget deficits because it diverts public attention away from what they are really responsible for—monetary policy. Perhaps so. But the presence of the deficit did make the Fed's job more difficult. With a miscalculation, it could release too much money into the economy and "monetize" the debt issued by the government. That's another way of saying that the Fed would be opening the monetary spigots and inviting more inflation.

What Volcker did from 1979 to 1982 was quite simple. He put the nation through a recession with tight money to control inflation. But to dismiss it as a mere clinical exercise is to forget the ingeniousness of the strategy, the stops and starts, the enormous political pressures, the mistakes and misreadings, and the tenacity of a very shrewd Federal Reserve chairman.

"He put the cork on inflation," said Secretary of State George Shultz.

"He made a stand against inflation at a time when he had a permissive administration," said economist Allen Sinai of Shearson Lehman Brothers. "The choice of tight money was the right one to counter the economic, political, and social demise of the country. I doubt that it could have been much better. One could argue that they put more slack into the economy than they should have, but I still give Volcker and the Fed an A-plus."

Alan Greenspan, the man named to succeed Volcker, said that he gave the Volcker board "substantial" credit for controlling inflation, but he added that "how much is not as yet clear. A substantial part also reflected the sharp rise in the value of the dollar, and that in turn was an interest-rate phenomenon to a certain extent. When people say the Fed was too tight during the recession, I adjust informed opinion for the rate of operations. It is extremely rare that you will get a consensus that the Federal Reserve is too easy during a recession, nor will you get a concern that it is too tight during an inflation. I would say, during this very unstable period from 1979 to 1984, they did a good deal better than average."

Greenspan's cautious assessment of the Volcker years stems from many years of economic analysis and from the knowledge that policies are best viewed with a few years of hindsight. The economic slack created by Volcker's policies did wipe out most of the residual inflation left over from the 1970s. The problem with this inflation was that it kept spiraling upward in the form of wage and price increases and was being built into expectations. Shock treatment seemed to be a good, credible cure.

But, as Volcker himself has warned, inflation has a way of worming its way back into the system, just as prices began to take off again early in 1987 as a result of a falling dollar. Keeping inflation under 4 percent for four years in a row was a major accomplishment, but if prices quickly rose much higher than 4 percent, he felt it would be destructive psychologically to a nation that had suffered economically to get price increases under control.

Volcker's critics on both the left and right make essentially the same argument—that inflation did not have to be knocked in the head so abruptly. Milton Friedman, the monetarist economist and constant Fed critic, said that the gradualist approach would have worked if the Fed had given up its temptation to fine-tune the economy. Former Fed member Nancy Teeters said that tight-money policy was too severe and did not sufficiently recognize that high oil prices played a big role in the inflationary surge. Inflation began to subside as oil prices came down, she noted.

The lesson of the 1979–1982 period is that Volcker did not take Fed policy into an extremist world, although at times some said it skirted the fringes. At the beginning, he was being cheered on by the politicians. When the recession came and political leaders began to squeal and threaten the Fed's independence, the central bank moved toward accommodation. It happened, of course, that inflation had been brought under control at that point. What should be said about this is that the possible course for the Fed to take was pretty wide. It chose an extremely tight course, hoping to crack inflation early. Volcker plotted his strategy carefully, stumbling only occasionally, and came out with a triumph.

The plan he used, trying to keep the Federal Reserve from exceeding a certain percentage of money growth each year, minimized political pressure on the central bank and enabled him to drive up interest rates higher than he ever would have dreamed.

In the end, though, Volcker tossed monetarism aside. It worked for a while and might, at some point in the future, be a useful method for tackling another bout of inflation, said former Fed official Tony Solomon.

In February 1987, the Federal Reserve declared M1, the basic measurement of money, persona non grata. It told Congress it wasn't going to follow a specific target for M1, as it had done on almost a mechanistic basis from 1979 to 1982. The relationship between money growth and economic growth had broken down. As a result, the Fed let M1 grow well beyond previous targets. Some, like Senator William Proxmire (D., Wisconsin), felt this was a terrible mistake and would sooner or later lead to an inflationary spiral.

The Fed took other economic indicators into account in deciding whether to loosen or tighten, but there was no single rule that guided its operations. The monetarists in particular wanted a hard-and-fast guideline for the Fed's internal operating procedure, feeling that this would enhance confidence in money and help foster growth and lower interest rates.

Volcker wanted a rule, too, but said he could find none that would satisfactorily do the job. All the possible guidelines had flaws. The only one left was discretion to evaluate the various indicators and use individual judgment on which way to proceed.

That's what economists meant when they said the country ran on a Volcker standard during his term in office. The value of our money depended on his experience, his training, his contacts, his biases, his philosophy about the economy, his reading of the political winds, and his day-to-day evaluation of economic and financial trends.

This is a lot of faith to place in one man. The record reveals that, on balance, Paul Volcker was true to that faith.

14
THE GREENSPAN ERA
BEGINS

Paul Volcker's real swan song as chairman of the Federal Reserve Board was delivered two years before he actually departed. It came on June 6, 1985, before the Harvard Alumni Association.

Upon examination, it was a lament.

"We continue to build more new offices than we can occupy," he said. "We've become expert in trading all kinds of financial assets and companies; we build hotels, attend conventions, and travel at home and abroad in unprecedented amounts—but all the while productivity lags.

"We spend our days issuing debt and retiring equity— both in record volume—and then we spend our evenings raising each other's eyebrows with gossip about signs of stress in the financial system.

"We rail at government inefficiency and intrusion in our markets—while we call upon the same government to protect our interests, our industry, and our financial institutions.

"And the best of our young gravitate toward Wall Street instead of Washington, our state houses, or our courthouses. Or, perhaps more accurately, a great many of them do end up in Washington—to run a lobby or represent a client."

In the course of the speech, Volcker warned that the United States needed a new commitment to maintain price stability, fight protectionism, and defend the dollar. "The dollar, like it or not, serves as the principal trading currency for the world and as an important store of value. There is no effective substitute available. How can we build a stable international system on an unstable currency—and how could we lead politically as well as economically?"

He criticized American economic education, saying international economics is relegated to the back of the book "with the implication the topic can be dropped if the semester isn't long enough. But there really are no separate compartments of 'domestic' and 'international' economics; as Gertrude Stein might have said, economics is economics is economics."

He closed his lament by pointing out how the world had changed. A new generation of financiers had grown up since he was a young man, he said, and it did not have the same fear of debt and leverage that previous ones did. The federal financial "safety net," such as the FDIC and the Fed, may be insufficient to deal with some of the excesses, he pointed out. He spoke of greed and selfishness and the need to control in some way "our acquisitive instincts" for the good of all. Finally, he said the notion of public service in the United States had declined, which meant to him that respect for government had declined, too.

It wasn't intended to be a swan song, but it was. It came from Volcker's heart.

The high-mindedness of this speech contrasted sharply with the government that surrounded him in Washington—the laissez-faire attitude of the Reagan administration, the willingness to minimize debt, and the declining value of the dollar. Reagan and his closest people were comfortable with the acquisitive set; in fact, his entire economic policy was all about making it possible for people to make a lot of money in America again without burdensome taxation or regulation.

Don Regan, the Wall Street executive who served as Reagan's Treasury Secretary and then chief of staff before being forced out, epitomized this attitude. Regan and Volcker not only disliked each other for personal reasons, they did not see eye to eye on deep philosophical questions about the role of government in the economy.

When Regan became White House chief of staff at the beginning of the president's second term, Volcker began preparing himself for the time when he would leave the job. Originally, he had thought he would stay only a couple of years; the massive debt and currency problems made him stretch his stay.

He kept hearing the rumors that as long as Regan had the president's ear, he had absolutely no chance of another term in office. There was even one report that Regan had extracted a promise from Reagan that Volcker would not be reappointed to a third term. Then the Iran-contra affair broke in late 1986, and Regan was forced out early in 1987, to be replaced by former Senator Howard Baker (R., Tennessee). Everyone suddenly thought that Volcker would be reappointed.

By that time, however, Volcker was not even sure he wanted another term. He had become sensitive to the financial needs of his family and strains of the physical separation from his wife.

One thing for sure. He was not going to the White House on hands and knees to beg for another term. Once he told Congress: "I don't seek jobs," and he meant it. He had been through too much for Ronald Reagan. He had taken the heat for battling inflation, including surviving the constant sniping by administration officials. He had fumed silently when the administration would not even consider his recommended appointments to the Fed and picked its own candidates based on political motivation.

He had rescued them from a debt crisis that could have become a disaster; in 1982, when Mexico nearly defaulted, the White House had no idea of the severity of the problem. He had warned about the deficit, and that had been resented.

Reagan's friends in the financial community were ganging up on Volcker, too. Many of them did not like Volcker's resistance to their expansion plans and his constant jawboning to get them to give another million or two for Mexico or Brazil or Argentina. He still had many friends in the banking community, but the enemies list was growing. A philosophical clash was beginning to swell up. Volcker feared that if banks got too far away from traditional banking and into all sorts of new financial ventures, it would harm the entire system. But others thought that these restrictions were harming U.S. banks internationally and keeping them smaller and weaker in relation to Japanese banks.

The debt crisis was becoming a tedious, difficult process, and Volcker especially had not made himself popular there. He sensed that those involved were getting fatigued with the difficult negotiations, and he was getting fatigued, too. It was getting increasingly time consuming.

Then there was the deficit. He had talked and talked about the dangers of the deficit until he was blue in the face. If he had shown the slightest bit of sanguinity about the deficit during his eight years in office, Congress would never have moved an inch. That it had moved some should have been a comfort to him, but Volcker was growing weary of preaching.

He preached again in February of 1987 when he delivered the Fed's annual Humphrey-Hawkins testimony, outlining the central bank's monetary policy for the year ahead. When he got back to his office that day, he said the appearance had bored him. He had played the same record over and over.

What about another term? I once asked him. "That ain't my life's ambition," he said.

And what was his ambition? He surely wanted to

make some money for once in his life; if a flash in the pan like David Stockman could pull in a million dollars, he should be able to do that, too. But Volcker didn't lust after the super-salaries he saw in the financial world. It was not part of his upbringing or of his being. His wife said that perhaps he could find a rundown hospital to straighten out.

In January or February, Volcker thought a lot about whether he wanted another term. If President Reagan had really wanted him, this would have been the time. His presidency was crumbling, the dollar was in a state of crisis, and he needed to see some sense of stability restored. Many market participants said Reagan could have helped himself by announcing immediately that Volcker was going to get a third term. But Reagan waited and waited, and Volcker would have been justified in coming to the conclusion that the president did not want him to continue.

Although Volcker said it was time for him to go when he announced his resignation after a meeting with the president on June 2, the president clearly could have persuaded him to remain for another term. Volcker would have accepted it reluctantly, because his sense of public service is great.

A week before the announcement, Volcker talked to chief of staff Howard Baker and said he wanted out. Baker asked him to reconsider; though he had criticized Volcker in the past, he respected the Fed chief. The next day, Volcker went fishing in Pennsylvania to wrestle with Baker's request. He returned on Saturday, went to New York to see his wife, and came back on Monday for a meeting with the president.

In the presence of Howard Baker and Jim Baker, he told the president of his decision to leave. Reagan did not try to dissuade him and said he respected the chairman's decision. The matter was settled orally. On his way out the door, Volcker pulled a letter out of his pocket. "Here, you might want this," he told the president. It was his letter of resignation.

His wife Barbara said Volcker agonized long and hard

over whether or not to stay. It was hard to let go after so many years in the limelight. Volcker had mixed feelings. "I didn't know he was going to resign until the day he did it," she said.

The next day, Reagan announced Volcker's resignation and Alan Greenspan's appointment. Greenspan said it took him "milliseconds" to accept.

One rumor spread in the aftermath of Volcker's resignation—that he was deeply concerned about his health. His wife said that was false. True, the chairman had stopped smoking his cigars a few months earlier, but that was because of constant nagging by his daughter and out of a feeling it would be more healthful. It might have stemmed from the fact that his daughter had been pushing him to get more insurance and he had to get a physical checkup. According to his wife, he passed the checkup. The rumor that Volcker was concerned about his health was, in the mind of some, a cover for Reagan's lack of enthusiasm for a third Volcker term.

When the change was announced, the dollar dropped rapidly, but then it recovered all its losses in a few days. From his standpoint, Reagan had chosen a good time to replace Volcker. The dollar had apparently bottomed out after several tumultuous months. The turmoil had ended at that moment.

Greenspan, a Wall Street economic consultant, was selected because he had a good reputation in the markets and because he was, like Volcker, flexible on monetary questions.

Greenspan has always been, like Arthur Burns before him, a political animal. He served on President Reagan's economic advisory board and advised the president during the 1980 campaign. He was one of the architects of the 1980 economic speech by Reagan in which he promised spending cuts and a balanced budget within four years. It didn't quite work out that way, but Greenspan showed he had influence with the president.

The economic advisory board had several monetarists, including Milton Friedman and Walter Wriston. Volcker was a frequent target of its criticism, although Greenspan often defended the Fed chief against the more ideological critics. Volcker went to a few meetings at Burns's insistence, but mostly just listened.

As Ford's chief economic advisor, Greenspan was good at finding compromises with Congress and within the administration over economic policy. As chairman of the commission that forged a plan to save the Social Security system from bankruptcy, he helped to bring competing sides together.

In the instant analysis that followed Greenspan's selection, it was often suggested that he would not be as tough as Volcker when the White House put the pressure on and that he would, in an election year, expand the money supply to take care of whoever the Republican presidential nominee is.

There was never anything factual for one to draw such a conclusion, except that Greenspan maintained his Republican political friendships and worked for two GOP presidents, Nixon and Ford. These associations left Greenspan with the job of convincing the markets, just as any other Fed chairman must, that he is serious about controlling inflation and maintaining the dollar's stability. His speeches and statements of the past indicate that he has economic instincts similar to Volcker's—flexible, with an understanding of the politics of the Fed.

His assessment of the Volcker years may provide some clues to his own future with the Fed. In an interview a few months before Greenspan was selected, he said that if the Fed under Volcker had truly focused only on the money supply and not tried to influence the federal funds rate at all, it would have been "an extraordinary revolution." In this sense, the Fed under Volcker was never 100 percent monetarist, he noted. It did keep some control over interest rates—just not as much as before.

"The Fed obviously and significantly used the federal funds rate as a policy guide," he said. "They didn't wholly go to a monetary aggregate [money supply] system. The crucial issue of Federal Reserve policy is always the trade-off between the funds rate and the monetary aggregates. In a sense, they work together. The way you affect the funds rate is by adjusting the supply of reserves to the system. To the extent you create excessive reserves in the system, you will expand the money supply, and to the extent that you try to hold the short-term rate structure down, that implies expansion of the money supply. Conversely, and in that sense, what the Fed cannot do is work outside the functions of the market. That means it can only affect short-term interest rates in the short run, but it cannot in the long run. The Fed cannot affect interest rates over a two- or three-year period. It can for a two- or three-week period. The short-term [interest] rate in the short run is determined by the supply and demand for reserves. In the longer term, it is also affected by inflation premiums embodied in the interest-rate structure. While the Fed can temporarily drive short-term interest rates down, if it does so by an excessive growth in the money supply, it will turn out to be self-defeating."

The foregoing is indicative of Greenspan's thinking and rhetoric. His knowledge of the subject is deep and he well understands the main pitfalls of Federal Reserve policy, which is at least half the battle. The trick is knowing what is excessive and what is not.

When I noted in my question to him that there is a conflict over the Volcker era in the erratic way in which the Fed supplied monetary reserves to the banking system, Greenspan responded:

"The fact that there is that conflict among those who are doing the evaluation suggests that they as a board were very sensitive to how they would be perceived. The Federal Reserve is, despite its independence, a political institution. It is not unaware of the extent to which the Congress and/or the presidency is reacting to the board. What they endeavor to do is to swing policy within the range of certain parameters. They get neither extremely tight nor extremely easy. In today's world, having been through the 1970s inflation, there would be a tendency to be tighter than one would have been in the 1950s or 1960s. The fact that the Volcker board is being attacked by both sides is suggestive of the fact that they have skillfully maintained—at least from a political point of view—a policy which is not perceived as going outside the consensus of the analysts in the world."

He said he gave the Volcker board credit for solving the inflation of the 1970s "to a substantial extent. How much is not clear. A substantial part of it was reflected in the rise of the dollar. That, in turn, was an interest-rate phenomenon to a certain extent."

All the evidence from Greenspan's past suggests that he regards inflation as evil—and that excessive growth in the money supply can reignite it quickly. As a young man, he was a disciple of novelist Ayn Rand, who wrote that if people act out of "rational selfishness," society and the economy will be better off. Greenspan was near-libertarian in his views in the 1960s, although he has moderated them today.

He is widely regarded by his colleagues as "one of the best nuts-and-bolts economists in America," as one put it. One of his big complaints has been the inadequacy of much of the government's data about the economy.

Volcker and Greenspan have known each other since the 1950s and were casual friends, though never close. But there is little question that the former Fed chairman respects Greenspan's ability.

With Greenspan's appointment, Reagan achieved something rare. He named every member of the board in his eight years in office. The board of governors does not come from the same old-boy network that it once did under past Fed chairmen. Reagan (or, more correctly, Reagan's advisors) took more of a political interest in the central bank and was determined to break it loose from the cautious bureaucratic agency it had been in the past.

Volcker went into office initially because the banking

system community, seeking a savior, found him to be the most attractive candidate and pushed him on President Carter. In 1987, the banking system—seeking to expand in many ways—no longer wanted Volcker. He had stepped on too many toes.

Greenspan comes from a different background—economic consulting and forecasting. He sits on several corporate boards and was always closer to the "real" economy, as opposed to the financial one, than was Paul Volcker. It is only guesswork, of course, but one could speculate that Greenspan's appointment represents something of a triumph of commercial interests over financial interests.

One can only guess what the Greenspan era will bring. If he is correct in his own assessment of past Federal Reserves, he too will drive policy between the boundaries of political acceptability.

Volcker crossed over those boundaries on several occasions when he tackled the inflation of the 1970s, and he won. Wherever he goes, people stop him and thank him for making their dollars worth something again. Perhaps that is an exaggeration, but most compliments are distortions of reality.

Volcker's legacy:

1. Inflation was held under 4 percent for four straight years.

2. Inflation can be conquered without killing the American economy.

3. The United States no longer can run an isolationist economic policy.

4. The dollar is the world's most important price; guard its value carefully.

5. The Federal Reserve Board should not be brought under political control; Volcker's experience in conquering inflation showed the wisdom of independence.

6. The Fed chief is a power in his own right in Washington, not an economic mechanic.

7. Finally, tight money may be the worst way on the face of the earth to fight inflation, except for all other ways.

Once when I confronted Volcker with a charge from a liberal economist that he was beginning to sound too much like a conservative German central banker with an excessive fear of inflation, he didn't hesitate: "I don't take that as criticism. That's a compliment. I'm in pretty good company there."

BIBLIOGRAPHY

de Saint Phalle, Thibaut. *The Federal Reserve, An Intentional Mystery*. New York: Praeger Publishers, 1985.

Galbraith, John Kenneth. *The Age of Uncertainty*. Boston: Houghton Mifflin Co., 1977.

Heilbroner, Robert L. *The Worldly Philosophers*. New York: Simon and Schuster, 1953.

Jones, David M. *Fed Watching*. New York Institute of Finance, 1986.

Kettl, Donald F. *Leadership at the Fed*. New Haven: Yale University, 1986.

Kraft, Joseph. *The Mexican Rescue*. New York: Group of Thirty, 1984.

Lekakachman, Robert. *The Age of Keynes*. New York: Random House, 1966.

Miller, Roger LeRoy, and Williams, Raburn M. *The New Economics of Richard Nixon*. New York: Harper's Magazine Press, 1972.

Roosa, Robert. *The United States and Japan in the International Monetary System, 1946–1985*. New York: Group of Thirty, 1986.

Safire, William. *Before the Fall.* Garden City, N.Y.: Doubleday and Company, 1975.

Schmidt, Helmut. *A Grand Strategy for the West.* New Haven and London: Yale University Press, 1985.

Shultz, George P., and Dam, Kenneth. *Economic Policy Beyond the Headlines.* New York: W. W. Norton & Co., 1977.

Solomon, Robert. *The International Monetary System, 1945–1976.* New York: Harper & Row, 1977.

Stein, Herbert. *Presidential Economics.* New York: Simon and Schuster, 1984.

Stockman, David. *The Triumph of Politics.* New York: Harper & Row, 1986.

Wriston, Walter B. *Risk and Other Four-Letter Words.* New York: Harper & Row, 1986.

Zweig, Phillip L. *Belly Up: The Collapse of the Penn Square Bank.* New York: Fawcett Columbine, 1985.